Pulpit Outlines
www.pulpitoutlines.com

52 Sermons About Jesus
By Barry L. Davis, D.Min.

Copyright©2013 Barry L. Davis

All Scripture taken from the King James Version.

Dear Fellow Preacher,

For most of us, one of the most rewarding, yet difficult tasks, is preparing messages to preach and teach. We are honored by God to stand before our congregation each week, and we want to give them the very best, but with the press of the many demands of ministry, sometimes that is difficult to do.

And if you're like me, you prefer writing your own sermons because you have a special connection with your congregation that is hard to reach through a message someone else has written. In other words, no one knows your people like you do!

Our new Pulpit Outline Series gives you a starting point – a sermon title, a deductive sermon outline; and a relevant illustration you can use however you like.

But you are free to "fill-in-the-blanks" so to speak, and add your own meat and potatoes to the mix! We invite you to make these messages your own, because only you know the people God has called you to preach to.

And we are so honored that you've invested in our very first volume in the Pulpit Outline series – *52 Sermons About Jesus* – there will be more to come!

May God Bless You as You Share His Word!

In Christ,
Barry L. Davis

www.pastorshelper.com I www.pulpitoutlines.com

Table of Contents

1. BEHOLD THE LAMB OF GOD

ILLUSTRATION:

[1]If you go over to Scotland, or anywhere there are lots of sheep, sooner or later you're going to see a very unusual sight. You'll see a little lamb running around the field, and you'll notice this lamb has what looks like an extra fleece tied around its back. In fact, you'll see there are little holes in the fleece for its four legs and usually a hole for its head. If you see a little lamb running around like that, that usually means its mother has died.

And without the protection and nourishment of a mother, any orphaned lamb will die. If you take the orphaned lamb and try to introduce it to another mother, the new mother will butt it away. She won't recognize the lamb's scent and will know the new baby is not one of her own lambs.

But thankfully, most flocks are large enough that there is a ewe that has recently lost a lamb. The shepherd will skin the dead lamb and make its fleece into a covering for the orphaned lamb, then he'll take the orphaned lamb to the mother whose baby just died. Now, when she sniffs the orphaned lamb, she will smell the fleece of her own lamb. Instead of butting the lamb away, she will accept it as one of her own.

In a similar way, we have become acceptable to God by being clothed with Christ.

1. THE LAMB OF GOD PROPHESIED

---

[1] PETER GRANT, "IN WHAT WAY IS JESUS CHRIST DIFFERENT?"

And Abraham said, My son, God will provide himself a lamb for a burnt offering: so they went both of them together. – Gen. 22:8

2. THE LAMB OF GOD TYPIFIED

Your lamb shall be without blemish, a male of the first year: ye shall take it out from the sheep, or from the goats: And ye shall keep it up until the fourteenth day of the same month: and the whole assembly of the congregation of Israel shall kill it in the evening. – Exo. 12:5-6

3. THE LAMB OF GOD IDENTIFIED

The next day John seeth Jesus coming unto him, and saith, Behold the Lamb of God, which taketh away the sin of the world. – John 1:29

4. THE LAMB OF GOD CRUCIFIED

He was oppressed, and he was afflicted, yet he opened not his mouth: he is brought as a lamb to the slaughter, and as a sheep before her shearers is dumb, so he openeth not his mouth. – Isaiah 53:7

5. THE LAMB OF GOD SATISFIED

Let us be glad and rejoice, and give honour to him: for the marriage of the Lamb is come, and his wife hath made herself ready. – Rev. 19:7

And there came unto me one of the seven angels which had the seven vials full of the seven last plagues, and talked with me, saying, Come hither, I will shew thee the bride, the Lamb's wife. – Rev. 21:9

6. THE LAMB OF GOD MAGNIFIED

Saying with a loud voice, Worthy is the Lamb that was slain to receive power, and riches, and wisdom, and strength, and honour, and glory, and blessing. – Rev. 5:12

7. THE LAMB OF GOD GLORIFIED

And I beheld, and, lo, in the midst of the throne and of the four beasts, and in the midst of the elders, stood a Lamb as it had been slain, having seven horns and seven eyes, which are the seven Spirits of God sent forth into all the earth. – Rev. 5:6

2. CHRIST – OUR EXAMPLE

For even hereunto were ye called: because Christ also suffered for us, leaving us an example, that ye should follow his steps. – 1 Peter 2:21

ILLUSTRATION:

[2]At the age of 23, Second Lieutenant Karl Marlantes was in charge of 40 marines during an intense battle in the Vietnam War. Marlantes had moved his men into the jungle as they waited for U.S. jets to bomb a hill that North Vietnamese soldiers had overtaken. Unfortunately, the jets came and dropped their bombs on the wrong hill. So when Marlantes led his men out of the jungle, they were instantly under fire from untouched machine-gun positions. Marlantes knew it would only take a few minutes before the enemy rockets and mortars found his troops. The entire mission ground to a halt as the U.S. soldiers ducked behind downed trees and huddled in shell holes.

Marlantes knew what he had to do next. He writes:

If I didn't get up and lead, we'd get wiped out …. I did a lot of things that day … but the one I'm most proud of is that I simply stood up, in the middle of that flying metal, and started up the hill …. I simply ran forward up the steep hill, zigzagging for the bunker, all by myself, hoping [my own soldiers] wouldn't hit me in the back. It's hard to zigzag while running uphill loaded down with ammunition and grenades.

---

[2] KARL MARLANTES, "THE TRUTH ABOUT BEING A HERO," *The Wall Street Journal* (8-20-11)

But then in the midst of his solo charge up the hill to take out the enemy, Marlantes suddenly saw some movement in his peripheral vision:

It was a marine! He was about 15 meters below me, zigzagging, falling, up and running again. Immediately behind him a long ragged line of Marines came moving and weaving up the hill behind me. Behind the line were spots of crumpled bodies, lying where they'd been hit. They'd all come with me .... Everyone was intermingled, weaving, rushing and covering, taking on each hole and bunker one at a time in groups .... WE, the group, just rushed forward all at once. WE couldn't be stopped. Just individuals among us were stopped ... but WE couldn't be .... I was we, no longer me.

1. IN LOVING

Jesus knowing that the Father had given all things into his hands, and that he was come from God, and went to God. – John 13:3

2. IN RECEIVING

Wherefore receive ye one another, as Christ also received us to the glory of God. – Romans 15:7

3. IN FORGIVING

Forbearing one another, and forgiving one another, if any man have a quarrel against any: even as Christ forgave you, so also do ye. – Col. 3:13

3. CHRIST OUR POWER – PART 1

ILLUSTRATION:

[3]Tim Keller tells the following story about the power of Christ's resurrection:

A minister was in Italy, and there he saw the grave of a man who had died centuries before who was an unbeliever and completely against Christianity, but a little afraid of it too. So the man had a huge stone slab put over his grave so he would not have to be raised from the dead in case there is a resurrection from the dead. He had insignias put all over the slab saying, "I do not want to be raised from the dead. I don't believe in it." Evidently, when he was buried, an acorn must have fallen into the grave. So a hundred years later the acorn had grown up through the grave and split that slab. It was now a tall towering oak tree. The minister looked at it and asked, "If an acorn, which has power of biological life in it, can split a slab of that magnitude, what can the acorn of God's resurrection power do in a person's life?"

Keller comments:

The minute you decide to receive Jesus as Savior and Lord, the power of the Holy Spirit comes into your life. It's the power of the resurrection – the same thing that raised Jesus from the dead …. Think of the

---

[3] NANCY GUTHRIE, EDITOR, *Jesus, Keep Me Near the Cross* (CROSSWAY, 2009), P. 136

things you see as immovable slabs in your life—your bitterness, your insecurity, your fears, your self-doubts. Those things can be split and rolled off. The more you know him, the more you grow into the power of the resurrection.

1. THE POWER OF HIS RESURRECTION

That I may know him, and the power of his resurrection, and the fellowship of his sufferings, being made conformable unto his death. – Phil. 3:10

2. THE POWER OF HIS GRACE

And he said unto me, My grace is sufficient for thee: for my strength is made perfect in weakness. Most gladly therefore will I rather glory in my infirmities, that the power of Christ may rest upon me. – 2 Cor. 12:9

3. THE POWER OF HIS SPIRIT

That he would grant you, according to the riches of his glory, to be strengthened with might by his Spirit in the inner man; That Christ may dwell in your hearts by faith; that ye, being rooted and grounded in love. – Eph. 3:16-17

4. THE POWER OF HIS PRESERVATION

Blessed be the God and Father of our Lord Jesus Christ, which according to his abundant mercy hath begotten us again unto a lively hope by the resurrection of Jesus Christ from the dead, To an inheritance incorruptible, and undefiled, and that fadeth not away, reserved in heaven for you, Who are kept by the power of God through faith unto salvation ready to be revealed in the last time. – 1 Peter 1:3-5

5. THE POWER OF HIS LOVE

According as his divine power hath given unto us all things that pertain unto life and godliness, through the knowledge of him that hath called us to glory and virtue. – 2 Peter 1:3

4. CHRIST OUR POWER – PART 2

ILLUSTRATION:

[4]"Faith is confidence in the person of Jesus Christ and in his power, so that even when his power does not serve my end, my confidence in him remains because of who he is." -- Ravi Zacharias

1. THE POWER OF HIS MINISTRY

But ye shall receive power, after that the Holy Ghost is come upon you: and ye shall be witnesses unto me both in Jerusalem, and in all Judaea, and in Samaria, and unto the uttermost part of the earth. – Acts 1:8

And when Peter saw it, he answered unto the people, Ye men of Israel, why marvel ye at this? or why look ye so earnestly on us, as though by our own power or holiness we had made this man to walk? – Acts 3:12

2. THE POWER OF HIS STRENGTH

For the which cause I also suffer these things: nevertheless I am not ashamed: for I know whom I have believed, and am persuaded that he is able to keep that which I have committed unto him against that day. – 2 Tim. 1:12

3. THE POWER OF HIS WORDS

---

[4] RAVI ZACHARIAS, *Jesus Among Other Gods* (THOMAS NELSON, 2002), P. 58

He that rejecteth me, and receiveth not my words, hath one that judgeth him: the word that I have spoken, the same shall judge him in the last day. – John 12:48

And they were all amazed, and spake among themselves, saying, What a word is this! for with authority and power he commandeth the unclean spirits, and they come out. And the fame of him went out into every place of the country round about. – Luke 4:36-37

4. THE POWER OF HIS GOSPEL

For I am not ashamed of the gospel of Christ: for it is the power of God unto salvation to every one that believeth; to the Jew first, and also to the Greek. For therein is the righteousness of God revealed from faith to faith: as it is written, The just shall live by faith. – Romans 1:16-17

5. THE POWER OF HIS PROMISES

Let not your heart be troubled: ye believe in God, believe also in me. In my Father's house are many mansions: if it were not so, I would have told you. I go to prepare a place for you. And if I go and prepare a place for you, I will come again, and receive you unto myself; that where I am, there ye may be also. – John 14:1-3

For all the promises of God in him are yea, and in him Amen, unto the glory of God by us. – 2 Cor. 1:20

5. CHRIST – OUR RANSOM

Who gave himself a ransom for all, to be testified in due time. – 1 Tim. 2:6

ILLUSTRATION:

[5]On a cold winter day Gabriel Estrada, a high school senior in Twin Lakes, Wisconsin, did the unthinkable. When his 17-year-old girlfriend secretly gave birth to a baby boy on January 15, 2002, she dressed it and asked him to deliver it to a church. Instead, Gabriel wrapped the baby in a canvas bag and left him in a portable toilet in a nearby park to die. But against incredible odds the baby was saved.

According to police there was virtually no chance the infant would survive. Temperatures were well below freezing. Lack of snow meant the nearby sledding hill would not be frequented by kids. And the sanitation company's scheduled pick-up at the port-a-potty was days away.

Village of Twin Lakes police credit a father and son for saving the child's life. About 4 o'clock in the afternoon on January 16th a father (wishing to remain anonymous) and his young son stopped at the abandoned West Side Park in need of a bathroom. Hearing a whimpering sound coming from the port-a-potty, they knew something was wrong. They called 911 to report what they had discovered.

When Officer Randy Prudik responded to the call, he pulled the canvas bag from the outdoor toilet and raced to

---

[5] MILWAUKEE JOURNAL SENTINEL (1-7-02)

nearby Burlington Memorial Hospital where the baby received emergency treatment.

"There's no way he would have survived that," Prudik said. "That little guy had somebody watching over him."

As a testament to the boy's survival, the nurses at the hospital dubbed him William Grant: William for the will to live and Grant for not taking life for granted.

On a grander scale, another Father and Son rescue team intervened on behalf of doomed humanity. (see John 3:16 below).

1. A RANSOM GIVEN AS A GIFT OF LOVE

For God so loved the world, that he gave his only begotten Son, that whosoever believeth in him should not perish, but have everlasting life. – John 3:16

2. A RANSOM GIVEN AS PAYMENT FOR OUR SIN

Grace be to you and peace from God the Father, and from our Lord Jesus Christ, Who gave himself for our sins, that he might deliver us from this present evil world, according to the will of God and our Father. – Gal. 1:3-4

Who gave himself for us, that he might redeem us from all iniquity, and purify unto himself a peculiar people, zealous of good works. – Titus 2:14

For he hath made him to be sin for us, who knew no sin; that we might be made the righteousness of God in him. – 2 Cor. 5:21

3. A RANSOM GIVEN AS OUR SUBSTITUTE

Even as the Son of man came not to be ministered unto, but to minister, and to give his life a ransom for many. – Matt. 20:28

I am the living bread which came down from heaven: if any man eat of this bread, he shall live for ever: and the bread that I will give is my flesh, which I will give for the life of the world. – John 6:51

4. A RANSOM GIVEN AS A REMBRANCE

And he took bread, and gave thanks, and brake it, and gave unto them, saying, This is my body which is given for you: this do in remembrance of me. Likewise also the cup after supper, saying, This cup is the new testament in my blood, which is shed for you. – Luke 22:19-20

6. CHRIST OUR SUBSTITUTE

ILLUSTRATION:

[6]In May 2009, my family was in Azusa, California, because one of our kids was graduating from Azusa Pacific University. My wife, Nancy, was going to speak at the commencement ceremonies, so she and I were invited to a special gathering of about 50 people—people from the graduating class of 50 years ago and a few faculty members. During the gathering, John Wallace, the president of APU, brought out three students who were graduating that year and told us that for the next two years, they were going to serve the poorest of the poor in India.

These three students thought they were there just to be commissioned and sent out with a blessing—which they were. But then something happened that they did not know was coming. John turned to them and said, "I have a piece of news for you. There's somebody you do not know—an anonymous donor—who is so moved by what you're doing that he has given a gift to this university in your name, on your behalf."

John turned to the first student and said, "You are forgiven your debt of $105,000." The kid immediately starts to cry. John turns to the next student: "You're forgiven your debt of $70,000." He then turns to the third student: "You are forgiven your debt of $130,000." All three students had no idea this was coming. They were just ambushed by grace—blown away that somebody they don't even know would pay their debt. The whole room was in tears.

---

[6] JOHN ORTBERG, IN THE SERMON "PATCH 'EM," MENLO PARK PRESBYTERIAN, MENLO PARK, CALIFORNIA (PREACHED 5-17-09)

1. HE WAS A CARING SUBSTITUTE

Surely he hath borne our griefs, and carried our sorrows: yet we did esteem him stricken, smitten of God, and afflicted. – Isaiah 53:4

2. HE WAS A WOUNDED SUBSTITUTE

But he was wounded for our transgressions, he was bruised for our iniquities: the chastisement of our peace was upon him; and with his stripes we are healed. – Isaiah 53:5

3. HE WAS A BRUISED SUBSTITUE

But he was wounded for our transgressions, he was bruised for our iniquities: the chastisement of our peace was upon him; and with his stripes we are healed. – Isaiah 53:5

4. HE WAS A GOD-PUNISHED SUBSTITUTE

All we like sheep have gone astray; we have turned every one to his own way; and the LORD hath laid on him the iniquity of us all. – Isaiah 53:6

5. HE WAS A SILENT SUBSTITUTE

He was oppressed, and he was afflicted, yet he opened not his mouth: he is brought as a lamb to the slaughter, and as a sheep before her shearers is dumb, so he openeth not his mouth. – Isaiah 53:7

6. HE WAS A SATISFIED SUBSTITUTE

He shall see of the travail of his soul, and shall be satisfied: by his knowledge shall my righteous servant justify many; for he shall bear their iniquities. – Isaiah 53:11

7. HE WAS A GOD-PLEASING SUBSTITUTE

Yet it pleased the LORD to bruise him; he hath put him to grief: when thou shalt make his soul an offering for sin, he shall see his seed, he shall prolong his days, and the pleasure of the LORD shall prosper in his hand. – Isaiah 53:10

8. HE WAS A SIN-BEARING SUBSTITUTE

Therefore will I divide him a portion with the great, and he shall divide the spoil with the strong; because he hath poured out his soul unto death: and he was numbered with the transgressors; and he bare the sin of many, and made intercession for the transgressors. – Isaiah 53:12

7. CHRIST THE COMING ONE

"And if I go and prepare a place for you, I will come again, and receive you unto myself; that where I am, there ye may be also." – John 14:3

ILLUSTRATION:

[7]In the 2007 film THE BUCKET LIST, two terminally ill men—played by Jack Nicholson and Morgan Freeman—take a road trip to do the things they always said they would do before they "kicked the bucket." In anticipation of the film's release, Nicholson was interviewed for an article in Parade magazine. While reflecting on his personal life, Nicholson said:

I used to live so freely. The mantra for my generation was "Be your own man!" I always said, "Hey, you can have whatever rules you want—I'm going to have mine. I'll accept the guilt. I'll pay the check. I'll do the time." I chose my own way. That was my philosophical position well into my 50s. As I've gotten older, I've had to adjust.

But reality has a way of getting the attention of even a Jack Nicholson. Later in the interview, Nicholson adds:

We all want to go on forever, don't we? We fear the unknown. Everybody goes to that wall, yet nobody knows what's on the other side. That's why we fear death.

---

[7] DOTSON RADER, "I WANT TO GO ON FOREVER," *Parade* MAGAZINE (12-9-07), PP. 6-8

1. THE PERSON

"I"

2. THE POWER

"I will."

3. THE PROMISE

"I will come."

4. THE PROSPECT

"I will come again."

5. THE PEOPLE

"And receive you unto myself."

6. THE PLACE

"That where I am."

7. THE PURPOSE

"There ye may be also."

8. WHAT CRUCIFIED JESUS?

ILLUSTRATION:

[8]Author Henri Nouwen tells the story of a family he knew in Paraguay. The father, a doctor, spoke out against the military regime there and its human rights abuses. Local police took their revenge on him by arresting his teenage son and torturing him to death. Enraged townsfolk wanted to turn the boy's funeral into a huge protest march, but the doctor chose another means of protest. At the funeral, the father displayed his son's body as he had found it in the jail—naked, scarred from electric shocks and cigarette burns, and beatings. All the villagers filed past the corpse, which lay not in a coffin but on the blood-soaked mattress from the prison. It was the strongest protest imaginable, for it put injustice on grotesque display.

Isn't that what God did at Calvary? ... The cross that held Jesus' body, naked and marked with scars, exposed all the violence and injustice of this world. At once, the cross revealed what kind of world we have and what kind of God we have: a world of gross unfairness, a God of sacrificial love.

1. BETRAYAL

And while he yet spake, lo, Judas, one of the twelve, came, and with him a great multitude with swords and staves, from the chief priests and elders of the people. Now he that betrayed him gave them a sign, saying, Whomsoever I

---

[8] PHILIP YANCEY, *Disappointment with God* (ZONDERVAN, 1997), PP. 185-186

shall kiss, that same is he: hold him fast. And forthwith he came to Jesus, and said, Hail, master; and kissed him. And Jesus said unto him, Friend, wherefore art thou come? Then came they, and laid hands on Jesus, and took him. – Matt. 26:47-50

2. FALSE TESTIMONY

Now the chief priests, and elders, and all the council, sought false witness against Jesus, to put him to death; But found none: yea, though many false witnesses came, yet found they none. At the last came two false witnesses. – Matt. 26:59-60

3. WICKEDNESS

Him, being delivered by the determinate counsel and foreknowledge of God, ye have taken, and by wicked hands have crucified and slain. – Acts 2:23

4. IGNORANCE

And now, brethren, I wot that through ignorance ye did it, as did also your rulers. But those things, which God before had shewed by the mouth of all his prophets, that Christ should suffer, he hath so fulfilled. – Acts 3:17-18

5. HATRED

Then Jesus said unto them, My time is not yet come: but your time is alway ready. The world cannot hate you; but me it hateth, because I testify of it, that the works thereof are evil. – John 7:6-7

6. MY SINS

But he was wounded for our transgressions, he was bruised for our iniquities: the chastisement of our peace was upon him; and with his stripes we are healed. – Isaiah 53:5

9. THE CHRIST LIFE

"I am come that they might have life, and that they might have it more abundantly." – John 10:10

ILLUSTRATION:

[9]Albert Pujols, the first baseman for the St. Louis Cardinals, is a World Series champ, an eight-time All Star, the recipient of three National League MVP awards, and according to a 2008 poll of 30 MLB managers, the most feared hitter in the sport. But even more impressive is his life off the field. The Pujols Family Foundation he started offers support and care to people with Down syndrome and their families, while also helping the poor in the Dominican Republic. He and his wife of ten years provide a loving household for four little children. But most importantly, he is a passionate disciple of Christ.

While speaking at an event at Lafayette Senior High School in Missouri, Pujols told the audience of men and young boys, "As a Christian, I am called to live a holy life. My standard for living is set by God, not by the world. I am responsible for growing and sharing the gospel." Then, after reading Paul's words in Philippians 2:3—"Do nothing out of selfish ambition or vain conceit, but in humility consider others better than yourselves"—Pujols told the crowd, "One way for me to stay satisfied in Jesus is for me to stay humble. Humility is getting on your knees and staying in God's will—what he wants for me, not what the world wants." He added: "It would be easy to go out and

---

[9] TIM ELLSWORTH, "HOLY HITTER," *World* MAGAZINE (2-27-10)

do whatever I want, but those things only satisfy the flesh for a moment. Jesus satisfies my soul forever."

1. LIFE FROM CHRIST

"Verily, verily, I say unto you, The hour is coming, and now is, when the dead shall hear the voice of the Son of God: and they that hear shall live." – John 5:25

2. LIFE IN CHRIST

For the law of the Spirit of life in Christ Jesus hath made me free from the law of sin and death. – Romans 8:2

3. LIFE WITH CHRIST

God is faithful, by whom ye were called unto the fellowship of his Son Jesus Christ our Lord. – 1 Cor. 1:9

4. LIFE TO CHRIST

And that he died for all, that they which live should not henceforth live unto themselves, but unto him which died for them, and rose again. – 2 Cor. 5:15

5. LIFE FOR CHRIST

I am crucified with Christ: nevertheless I live; yet not I, but Christ liveth in me: and the life which I now live in the flesh I live by the faith of the Son of God, who loved me, and gave himself for me. – Gal. 2:20

10. JESUS DID THIS FOR YOU!

ILLUSTRATION:

[10]The concept of substitution lies at the heart of both sin and salvation. For the essence of sin is man substituting himself for God, while the essence of salvation is God substituting himself for man. – John Stott

1. JESUS WAS THE GOD-PROVIDED SUBSTITUTE

But God commendeth his love toward us, in that, while we were yet sinners, Christ died for us. – Romans 5:8

2. JESUS WAS THE SIN-MADE SUBSTITUTE

For he hath made him to be sin for us, who knew no sin; that we might be made the righteousness of God in him. – 2 Cor. 5:21

3. JESUS WAS THE CURSE-BEARING SUBSTITUTE

Christ hath redeemed us from the curse of the law, being made a curse for us: for it is written, Cursed is every one that hangeth on a tree. – Gal. 3:13

---

[10] JOHN STOTT, *The Cross of Christ* (INTERVARSITY, 1986)

4. JESUS WAS THE LIFE-SACRIFICED SUBSTITUTE

Purge out therefore the old leaven, that ye may be a new lump, as ye are unleavened. For even Christ our passover is sacrificed for us. – 1 Cor. 5:7

5. JESUS WAS THE GRACE-IMPARTING SUBSTITUTE

What shall we then say to these things? If God be for us, who can be against us? He that spared not his own Son, but delivered him up for us all, how shall he not with him also freely give us all things? Who shall lay any thing to the charge of God's elect? It is God that justifieth. Who is he that condemneth? It is Christ that died, yea rather, that is risen again, who is even at the right hand of God, who also maketh intercession for us. – Romans 8:31-34

6. JESUS WAS THE HOLY-INSPIRING SUBSTITUTE

Hereby perceive we the love of God, because he laid down his life for us: and we ought to lay down our lives for the brethren. – 1 John 3:16

7. JESUS WAS THE GLORY-SECURING SUBSTITUTE

For if we believe that Jesus died and rose again, even so them also which sleep in Jesus will God bring with him. – 1 Thess. 4:14

11. CHRIST IS SUPERIOR

ILLUSTRATION:

[11]In July 2009, Parade magazine ran an article entitled, "The Race for the Secret of the Universe." It focused on Fermilab, a four-mile-round particle accelerator that resides west of Chicago. The scientists gathered there are searching for the ever-elusive Higgs boson, also known as "the God particle."

The article explains more: "Physicists believe that this special subatomic particle allows all of the other particles in the universe to have mass and come together to form, well, basically everything that is around us. [According to one Fermilab theorist], without so-called God particles .... 'atoms would have no integrity, so there would be no chemical bonding, no stable structures—no liquids or solids—and, of course, no physicists and no reporters.'"

While it's certainly possible that God built such a tiny particle into the deepest part of his creation, it isn't the God particle. The God particle that holds all things together— actually, the God person—is Jesus Christ. Consider what Paul writes in Ephesians 1:10: "[Christ] bring[s] unity to all things in heaven and on earth." Consider also Colossians 1:16: "for in [Christ] all things were created: things in heaven and on earth, visible and invisible, whether thrones or powers or authorities; all things have been created through him and for him."

1. IN EVERYTHING

---

[11] STEPHEN FORD, "THE RACE FOR THE SECRET OF THE UNIVERSE," *Parade* MAGAZINE (7-26-09), P.4

Who is the image of the invisible God, the firstborn of every creature. – Col. 1:15

2. IN CREATION

For by him were all things created, that are in heaven, and that are in earth, visible and invisible, whether they be thrones, or dominions, or principalities, or powers: all things were created by him, and for him. – Col. 1:16

3. IN ORDER

And he is before all things, and by him all things consist. – Col. 1:17

4. IN POWER

And he is before all things, and by him all things consist. – Col. 1:17

5. IN POSITION

And he is the head of the body, the church: who is the beginning, the firstborn from the dead; that in all things he might have the preeminence. – Col. 1:18

6. IN RESURRECTION

And he is the head of the body, the church: who is the beginning, <u>the firstborn from the dead</u>; that in all things he might have the preeminence. – Col. 1:18

7. IN CONTENT

For it pleased the Father that in him should all fulness dwell. – Col. 1:19

12. JESUS IS THE TRUTH

Jesus saith unto him, I am the way, the truth, and the life: no man cometh unto the Father, but by me." – John 14:6

ILLUSTRATION:

[12]Vishal Mangalwadi, a Christian scholar from India, shared the following story after visiting America:

In November, 2011, I visited two classes at a Christian university in North America. I asked both: "How many of you would still believe Christianity if you found out tomorrow that Christianity was not true. That is: God never became a man; Jesus did not die for our sin; or, that he did not rise from the dead?"

Twelve hands went up in [the class of about 25 students]. These sincere and devout students had grown up in Christian homes, gone to church all their lives, and studied in Christian schools. Some had been in that Christian university for three years! They respected their elders who taught them that Christianity was all about faith with little concern for truth.

Christianity lost America because 20th-century evangelicalism branded itself as the PARTY OF

---

[12] "WHY CHRISTIANITY LOST AMERICA?" *Vishal Mangalwadi's* BLOG (12-10-11)

FAITH. Secularism (science, university, media) became the PARTY OF TRUTH. This is one reason why 70 percent of Christian youth give up meaningful involvement with the church when they grow up.... Secularism acquired the "truth" brand by default because evangelicalism began defining the Church's mission as [just] cultivating FAITH, not [also] promoting knowledge of TRUTH.

1. JESUS IS THE TRUE LIGHT

In the beginning was the Word, and the Word was with God, and the Word was God. The same was in the beginning with God. All things were made by him; and without him was not any thing made that was made. In him was life; and the life was the light of men. – John 1:1-4

2. JESUS IS THE TRUE BREAD

Then Jesus said unto them, Verily, verily, I say unto you, Moses gave you not that bread from heaven; but my Father giveth you the true bread from heaven. For the bread of God is he which cometh down from heaven, and giveth life unto the world. – John 6:32-33

3. JESUS IS THE TRUE VINE

I am the true vine, and my Father is the husbandman. Every branch in me that beareth not fruit he taketh away: and every branch that beareth fruit, he purgeth it, that it may bring forth more fruit. – John 15:1-2

4. JESUS IS THE TRUE WITNESS

...These things saith the Amen, the faithful and true witness, the beginning of the creation of God. – Rev. 3:14b

5. JESUS IS THE TRUE GOD

And we know that the Son of God is come, and hath given us an understanding, that we may know him that is true, and we are in him that is true, even in his Son Jesus Christ. This is the true God, and eternal life. – 1 John 5:20

These shall make war with the Lamb, and the Lamb shall overcome them: for he is Lord of lords, and King of kings: and they that are with him are called, and chosen, and faithful. – Rev. 17:14

13. CHRIST THE OVERCOMER

These shall make war with the Lamb, and the Lamb shall overcome them... – Rev. 17:14a

ILLUSTRATION:

[13]William Gurnall, after encouraging believers to hold fast to the assurance that God is watching Satan's every move and will not let him have the final victory, writes, "When God says 'Stay!' [Satan] must stand like a dog by the table while the saints feast on God's comfort. He does not dare to snatch even a tidbit, for the Master's eye is always upon him." And so it is; our Master's eye is ever upon him. After his first act of obedience, his failure and doom were sealed.

1. JESUS HAS BRUISED THE SERPENT'S HEAD

And I will put enmity between thee and the woman, and between thy seed and her seed; it shall bruise thy head, and thou shalt bruise his heel. – Gen. 3:15

2. JESUS HAS BOUND THE STRONG MAN

---

[13] ERWIN LUTZER, *The Serpent of Paradise* (MOODY, 1996)

"But when a stronger than he shall come upon him, and overcome him, he taketh from him all his armour wherein he trusted, and divideth his spoils. He that is not with me is against me: and he that gathereth not with me scattereth." – Luke 11:22-23

3. JESUS HAS DESTROYED THE WORKS OF THE DEVIL

He that committeth sin is of the devil; for the devil sinneth from the beginning. For this purpose the Son of God was manifested, that he might destroy the works of the devil. – 1 John 3:8

4. JESUS HAS TRIUMPHED OVER PRINCIPALITIES AND POWERS

And having spoiled principalities and powers, he made a shew of them openly, triumphing over them in it. – Col. 2:15

5. JESUS HAS TAKEN AWAY THE POWER OF DEATH

Forasmuch then as the children are partakers of flesh and blood, he also himself likewise took part of the same; that through death he might destroy him that had the power of death, that is, the devil. – Heb. 2:14

6. JESUS HAS OVERCOME THE WORLD

"These things I have spoken unto you, that in me ye might have peace. In the world ye shall have tribulation: but be of good cheer; I have overcome the world." – John 16:33

14. JESUS IS THE WAY – PART 1

Jesus saith unto him, I am the way, the truth, and the life: no man cometh unto the Father, but by me." – John 14:6

ILLUSTRATION:

[14]Tiger Woods was put on the spot by an evangelical guest of Nike on October 9, 2006, during an exclusive golf outing for top business and entertainment executives.

That day, 30 people gathered at the Trump golf course in Los Angeles for the 2006 "Tee It up with Tiger Woods" event, which included a private golf session and lunch with the living legend. During the lunch, there was a question-and-answer session with Woods. Most people asked about their swings or golf questions.

However, one guest of Nike stood up and asked two questions: "Have you accepted Jesus as your Lord and Savior? And if not, prayerfully, would you?" A source present at the lunch later said: "You could have heard a pin drop. People were mortified. But Tiger was as unflappable as he is on the golf course."

Tiger said: "My father was a Christian—of course Christianity was part of my life. But my mother is Asian, and Buddhism was also part of my childhood. So I practice both faiths respectfully."

That might sound nice to some, but according to the Bible, there is only One Way!

---

[14] ELLIOT HARRIS, "WOODS TAKES EVANGELICAL TO SUNDAY SCHOOL," *Chicago Sun-Times* (10-19-06)

1. JESUS IS THE WAY TO PARDON

Be it known unto you therefore, men and brethren, that through this man is preached unto you the forgiveness of sins. – Acts 13:38

2. JESUS IS THE WAY TO PEACE

Therefore being justified by faith, we have peace with God through our Lord Jesus Christ: By whom also we have access by faith into this grace wherein we stand, and rejoice in hope of the glory of God. And not only so, but we glory in tribulations also: knowing that tribulation worketh patience; And patience, experience; and experience, hope: And hope maketh not ashamed; because the love of God is shed abroad in our hearts by the Holy Ghost which is given unto us. – Romans 5:1-5

3. JESUS IS THE WAY TO HOLINESS

But if we walk in the light, as he is in the light, we have fellowship one with another, and the blood of Jesus Christ his Son cleanseth us from all sin. – 1 John 1:7

4. JESUS IS THE WAY TO HAPPINESS

For I have given you an example, that ye should do as I have done to you. Verily, verily, I say unto you, The servant is not greater than his lord; neither he that is sent greater than he that sent him. If ye know these things, happy are ye if ye do them. – John 13:15-17

15. JESUS IS THE WAY – PART 2

Jesus saith unto him, I am the way, the truth, and the life: no man cometh unto the Father, but by me." – John 14:6

ILLUSTRATION:

[15]I was traveling on a plane from San Francisco to Los Angeles a few years ago. I was sitting next to the window, reading a Christian book. The man next to me, obviously from the Eastern hemisphere, asked, "Are you a religious man?" "Well, yes," I said. "I am too," he responded. We began talking about religion. In the middle of the conversation I asked, "Can you give me a one-liner that captures the essence of your faith?" "Well, yes," he said. "We are all part of the problem, and we are all part of the solution."

We talked about his one-liner, a statement I felt was very helpful. After a while I said, "Would you like a one-liner that captures the Christian faith?"

"Sure," he responded.

"We are all part of the problem, but there is only one man who is the solution. His name is JESUS."

1. JESUS IS THE WAY TO HEAVEN

Let not your heart be troubled: ye believe in God, believe also in me. In my Father's house are many mansions: if it

---

[15] ROBERT WEBBER, *Who Gets to Narrate the World?* (IVP, 2008), P. 26

were not so, I would have told you. I go to prepare a place for you. And if I go and prepare a place for you, I will come again, and receive you unto myself; that where I am, there ye may be also. – John 14:1-3

2. JESUS IS THE WAY TO GOD

For Christ also hath once suffered for sins, the just for the unjust, that he might bring us to God, being put to death in the flesh, but quickened by the Spirit. – 1 Peter 3:18

3. JESUS IS THE WAY TO ALL SPIRITUAL BLESSINGS

Blessed be the God and Father of our Lord Jesus Christ, who hath blessed us with all spiritual blessings in heavenly places in Christ: According as he hath chosen us in him before the foundation of the world, that we should be holy and without blame before him in love: Having predestinated us unto the adoption of children by Jesus Christ to himself, according to the good pleasure of his will, To the praise of the glory of his grace, wherein he hath made us accepted in the beloved. – Eph. 1:3-6

4. JESUS IS THE WAY TO THE GLORIES OF HEAVEN

He which testifieth these things saith, Surely I come quickly. Amen. Even so, come, Lord Jesus. – Rev. 22:20

16. JESUS IS THE WORD OF GOD

ILLUSTRATION:

[16]Jesus was the audible, visible Word who expressed the heart of the inaudible, invisible God. Jesus Christ is God's great Visual Aid.

Origen, in the third century, had a great analogy. He told of a village with a huge statue—so immense you couldn't see exactly what it was supposed to represent. Finally, someone miniaturized the statue so one could see the person it honored. Origen said, "That is what God did in his Son." Paul tells us Christ is the self-miniaturization of God, the visible icon or image of the invisible God (Colossians 1). In Christ we have God in a comprehensible way. In Christ we have God's own personal and definitive visit to the planet.

1. HIS ETERNITY

In the beginning was the Word, and the Word was with God, and the Word was God. – John 1:1

And he is before all things, and by him all things consist. – Col. 1:17

2. HIS EQUALITY

---

[16] DALE BRUNER, THEOLOGIAN, FROM "IS JESUS INCLUSIVE OR EXCLUSIVE?" *Theology, News, and Notes* OF FULLER SEMINARY (OCT. 1999), P.4

In the beginning was the Word, and <u>the Word was with God</u>, and the Word was God. – John 1:1

I and my Father are one. – John 10:30

3. HIS DEITY —

In the beginning was the Word, and the Word was with God, and <u>the Word was God</u>. – John 1:1

For in him dwelleth all the fulness of the Godhead bodily. – Col. 2:9

4. HIS HUMANITY —

And the Word was made flesh, and dwelt among us, (and we beheld his glory, the glory as of the only begotten of the Father,) full of grace and truth. – John 1:14

5. HIS TESTIMONY

No man hath seen God at any time; the only begotten Son, which is in the bosom of the Father, he hath declared him. – John 1:18

17. CHRIST IS WORTHY

ILLUSTRATION:

[17]We live in a fast-paced culture, but some things just ought to happen slowly.

The book FINAL SALUTE tells the story of Major Steve Beck, a U.S. Marine whose heart-wrenching task is to inform the nearest of kin when a Marine is killed in Iraq. Beck doesn't just break the sad news and then leave; for several days he may help the family through the process of the funeral. That includes supervising the Marine honor guard that stands near the fallen soldier's body.

The honor guard learns from Beck how to salute their fallen fellow-Marine as they leave or resume guard with a slow salute that isn't taught in basic training. The slow salute requires a three second raising of the hand to the head, a three second hold, and then a three second lowering of the hand—a gesture of respect that takes about nine times longer than normal. Beck explains: "A salute to your fallen comrade should take time."

Indeed, those who die serving their country are worthy of great honor, worthy of a slow salute, worthy of extra time. To do some things fast, just to get them done so we can move on to the next thing in our lives, sends a subtle message of disrespect.

---

[17] JIM SHEELER, *Final Salute* (PENGUIN, 2008); AS SEEN IN "DEATH COMES KNOCKING," *The Week* (5-23-08), P. 37

So it is with our worship of God. God deserves a slow salute. The Savior who gave his life for us is worthy of our time.

1. CHRIST IS WORTHY AS THE GOOD SHEPHERD

I am the good shepherd: the good shepherd giveth his life for the sheep. – John 10:11

2. CHRIST IS WORTHY AS LORD

Thou art worthy, O Lord, to receive glory and honour and power: for thou hast created all things, and for thy pleasure they are and were created. – Rev 4:11

3. CHRIST IS WORTHY AS OVERCOMER

And I saw in the right hand of him that sat on the throne a book written within and on the backside, sealed with seven seals. And I saw a strong angel proclaiming with a loud voice, Who is worthy to open the book, and to loose the seals thereof? And no man in heaven, nor in earth, neither under the earth, was able to open the book, neither to look thereon. And I wept much, because no man was found worthy to open and to read the book, neither to look thereon. And one of the elders saith unto me, Weep not: behold, the Lion of the tribe of Juda, the Root of David, hath prevailed to open the book, and to loose the seven seals thereof. And I beheld, and, lo, in the midst of the throne and of the four beasts, and in the midst of the elders, stood a Lamb as it had been slain, having seven horns and seven eyes, which are the seven Spirits of God sent forth into all the earth. And he came and took the book out of the right hand of him that sat upon the throne. And when he had taken the book, the four beasts and four and twenty elders fell down before the Lamb, having every one of them harps, and golden vials full of odours, which are the prayers of saints. And they sung a new song, saying, Thou art worthy to take the book, and to open the seals thereof: for thou wast slain, and hast redeemed us to God by thy blood out of every kindred, and tongue, and people, and nation. – Rev. 5:1-9

4. CHRIST IS WORTHY AS THE LAMB

Saying with a loud voice, Worthy is the Lamb that was slain to receive power, and riches, and wisdom, and strength, and honour, and glory, and blessing. – Rev. 5:12

18. JESUS DIDN'T JUST SAY IT – HE LIVED IT!

ILLUSTRATION:

[18]A few years ago, a missionary came to our church and told a beautiful story about sharing the gospel with a remote tribe in Papua New Guinea. At the end of the story this missionary said, "I should really give the credit to Vaughn, my former youth pastor who loved me and inspired me to live for Christ and share the gospel with others." The next week another guy came to our church and he challenged us to start sponsoring kids living in poverty. The second speaker also concluded by saying, "I'm involved in this ministry because of my youth pastor, a guy named Vaughn." I found out those guys were from the same youth group!

Then the next week another speaker named Dan told us about his ministry at a rescue mission in the inner city of L.A. After Dan's talk, I casually mentioned, "It was so weird: the last two weeks both of our speakers mentioned how much impact their youth pastor, Vaughn, had on them." Dan looked surprised and then he told me, "I know Vaughn. He's a pastor in San Diego now, and he takes people into the dumps in Tijuana where kids are picking through the garbage. I was just with Vaughn in Tijuana. We

---

[18] FRANCIS CHAN, "THINK HARD, STAY HUMBLE."

would walk in the city, and these kids would run up to him, and he would show such deep love and affection for them. He'd hug them and have gifts and food for them. He'd figure out how to get them showers. Francis, it was eerie: the whole time I was walking with Vaughn, I kept thinking, IF JESUS WAS ON EARTH, I THINK THIS IS WHAT IT WOULD FEEL LIKE TO WALK WITH HIM. He just loved everyone he ran into, and he would tell them about God. People were just drawn to his love and affection." And then Dan said this, "The day I spent with Vaughn was the closest thing I've ever experienced to walking with Jesus."

Hearing this made me think, Would anyone in their right mind say that about me? WOULD ANYONE SAY THAT ABOUT YOU? ... As I thought about all this, I prayed, "Lord, that's what I want. I don't want to be the best speaker in the world. That doesn't matter. I don't want to be the most intelligent person on the planet. That's not what I want to be known for. I want to be known for someone saying, "Wow, he's a lot like Jesus."

1. JESUS PURPOSED TO DO GOD'S WILL

Then said I, Lo, I come (in the volume of the book it is written of me,) to do thy will, O God. – Heb. 10:7

He went away again the second time, and prayed, saying, O my Father, if this cup may not pass away from me, except I drink it, thy will be done. – Matt 26:42

2. JESUS SPREAD GOD'S WORD

For I have given unto them the words which thou gavest me; and they have received them, and have known surely that I came out from thee, and they have believed that thou didst send me. – John 17:8

3. JESUS WALKED IN GOD'S WAYS

Ye men of Israel, hear these words; Jesus of Nazareth, a man approved of God among you by miracles and wonders and signs, which God did by him in the midst of you, as ye yourselves also know. – Acts 2:22

How God anointed Jesus of Nazareth with the Holy Ghost and with power: who went about doing good, and healing all that were oppressed of the devil; for God was with him. – Acts 10:38

4. JESUS FULFILLED GOD'S WORK

I have glorified thee on the earth: I have finished the work which thou gavest me to do. – John 17:4

When Jesus therefore had received the vinegar, he said, It is finished: and he bowed his head, and gave up the ghost. – John 19:30

5. JESUS REVEALED GOD'S WORTH

For God so loved the world, that he gave his only begotten Son, that whosoever believeth in him should not perish, but have everlasting life. – John 3:16

19. JESUS' AUTHORITY

ILLUSTRATION:

[19]A number of years ago, when I was playing in a friendly men's softball game, the umpire made a call that incensed our coach. My coach didn't agree with the ump's interpretation of a specific league rule. The game stopped, and a heated discussion ensued. Finally, the ump sighed as he pulled a rulebook from his back pocket and proceeded to read page 27, paragraph 3b, section 1.

"As you can clearly see," he concluded, "this rule means that my call must stand." Unconvinced, my coach yelled, "But you're not interpreting that rule correctly." To which the ump replied, "Uh, excuse me, I think I should know: I wrote the rulebook." After an awkward silence, my coach walked back to the bench, shaking his head and pointing to the ref as he told us, "Get ahold of that guy. He wrote the rulebook!"

Throughout his ministry, Jesus didn't just affirm and endorse the words of Scripture; he talked and acted like he had AUTHORED the Scriptures. He lived with the authority of the One who wrote the "rulebook."

1. JESUS HAD THE AUTHORITY TO LAY DOWN HIS LIFE

---

[19] MATT WOODLEY, *The Gospel of Matthew: God With Us* (INTERVARSITY PRESS, 2011), PP. 68-69

Therefore doth my Father love me, because I lay down my life, that I might take it again. No man taketh it from me, but I lay it down of myself. I have power to lay it down, and I have power to take it again. This commandment have I received of my Father. – John 10:17-18

2. JESUS HAD THE AUTHORITY TO FORGIVE SINS

But that ye may know that the Son of man hath power on earth to forgive sins, (then saith he to the sick of the palsy,) Arise, take up thy bed, and go unto thine house. And he arose, and departed to his house. But when the multitudes saw it, they marvelled, and glorified God, which had given such power unto men. – Matt. 9:6-8

3. JESUS HAD AUTHORITY OVER DEMONS

And they were all amazed, insomuch that they questioned among themselves, saying, What thing is this? what new doctrine is this? for with authority commandeth he even the unclean spirits, and they do obey him. – Mark 1:27

4. JESUS HAD AUTHORITY OVER SICKNESS

And he goeth up into a mountain, and calleth unto him whom he would: and they came unto him. And he ordained twelve, that they should be with him, and that he might send them forth to preach, And to have power to heal sicknesses, and to cast out devils. – Mark 3:13-15

5. JESUS HAD AUTHORITY TO JUDGE

And hath given him authority to execute judgment also, because he is the Son of man. – John 5:27

6. JESUS HAD AUTHORITY OVER ALL MEN

As thou hast given him power over all flesh, that he should give eternal life to as many as thou hast given him. – John 17:2

7. JESUS HAD AUTHORITY IN HEAVEN AND EARTH

And Jesus came and spake unto them, saying, All power is given unto me in heaven and in earth. – Matt. 28:18

20. WHAT JESUS LEFT HIS DISCIPLES

ILLUSTRATION:

[20]George Patten was an 8-year-old kid who told his friends he had shaken the hand of the new president. "Did not," they probably jeered. "Did so!" he probably shot back. And so it went, back and forth, back and forth, as it so often does with kids.

The new president little George Patten was talking about was Abraham Lincoln, and the year was 1861. George insisted that he'd shaken Lincoln's hand the year before in Springfield, Illinois, when George was with his father, a journalist. But the little boy's classmates just wouldn't believe him. Finally, George's teacher wrote a letter to President Lincoln to discover the truth. Surprisingly, Lincoln wrote back. His note was short and sweet:

Executive Mansion, March 19, 1861.

Whom it may concern,
I did see and talk with master George Evans Patten, last May, at Springfield, Illinois.
Respectfully, A Lincoln.

Sometimes it is hard to believe the places to which ordinary people can go—where they can find themselves, who they can meet. Take us, for example. We who are Christians are taught to see ourselves in a whole new way in the Bible. We have met Jesus! And He has promised us as His disciples many wonderful things.

---

[20] ASSOCIATED PRESS, "LINCOLN'S LETTER TO BOY GOES ON SALE," AOLNEWS.COM (11-17-09)

1. HIS EXAMPLE OF HUMILITY

If I then, your Lord and Master, have washed your feet; ye also ought to wash one another's feet. For I have given you an example, that ye should do as I have done to you. – John 13:14-15

2. HIS PROMISE OF A HOME

Let not your heart be troubled: ye believe in God, believe also in me. In my Father's house are many mansions: if *it were* not *so*, I would have told you. I go to prepare a place for you. And if I go and prepare a place for you, I will come again, and receive you unto myself; that where I am, *there* ye may be also. – John 14:1-3

3. HIS SPIRIT AS THEIR COMFORTER

And I will pray the Father, and he shall give you another Comforter, that he may abide with you for ever; Even the Spirit of truth; whom the world cannot receive, because it seeth him not, neither knoweth him: but ye know him; for he dwelleth with you, and shall be in you. I will not leave you comfortless: I will come to you. – John 14:16-18

4. HIS PEACE TO KEEP THEM FROM FEAR

Peace I leave with you, my peace I give unto you: not as the world giveth, give I unto you. Let not your heart be troubled, neither let it be afraid. – John 14:27

5. HIS JOY TO REMAIN WITH THEM

These things have I spoken unto you, that my joy might remain in you, and that your joy might be full. – John 15:11

21. CHRIST'S GETHSEMANE PRAYER

ILLUSTRATION:

[21]Dennis Corrigan: "Gethsemane teaches us that the kingdom of God is entered only through the denial of one's own will and the affirmation of the will of God. Therefore, the cross must stand central to an understanding of the kingdom. Since the essence of the kingdom is our obedience to the absolute will of God, we understand it only as we bring our own will to the foot of the cross. No self-will can live unchallenged in God's kingdom."

1. IT WAS A PRAYER OF HUMILITY

And he went forward a little, and <u>fell on the ground, and prayed</u> that, if it were possible, the hour might pass from him. – Mark 14:35

2. IT WAS A PRAYER OF FAMILIARITY

And he said, <u>Abba, Father</u>, all things are possible unto thee; take away this cup from me: nevertheless not what I will, but what thou wilt. – Mark 14:36

3. IT WAS A PRAYER OF LONELINESS

---

[21] DENNIS CORRIGAN IN BRIDGE BUILDER (NOV./DEC. 1988). CHRISTIANITY TODAY, VOL. 33, NO. 4.

And he cometh, and findeth them sleeping, and saith unto Peter, Simon, sleepest thou? couldest not thou watch one hour? – Mark 14:37

4. IT WAS A PRAYER OF EARNESTNESS

And being in an agony he prayed more earnestly: and his sweat was as it were great drops of blood falling down to the ground. – Luke 22:44

Who in the days of his flesh, when he had offered up prayers and supplications with strong crying and tears unto him that was able to save him from death, and was heard in that he feared. – Heb. 5:7

5. IT WAS A PRAYER OF PERSEVERANCE

And <u>again</u> he went away, and prayed, and <u>spake the same words</u>. – Mark 14:39

6. IT WAS A PRAYER OF RESIGNATION

And he said, Abba, Father, all things are possible unto thee; take away this cup from me: nevertheless <u>not what I will, but what thou wilt</u>. – Mark 14:36

7. IT WAS A PRAYER OF REASSURANCE

And there appeared an angel unto him from heaven, strengthening him. – Luke 22:43

22. WHAT JESUS SUFFERED AT THE CROSS

ILLUSTRATION:

[22]In her book *The God Who Hung on the Cross*, journalist Ellen Vaughn retells a gripping story of how the Gospel came to a small village in Cambodia. In September 1999 Pastor Tuy Seng (not his real name) traveled to Kampong Thom Province in northern Cambodia. Throughout that isolated area, most villagers had cast their lot with Buddhism or spiritism. Christianity was virtually unheard of.

But much to Seng's surprise, when he arrived in one small, rural village the people warmly embraced him and his message about Jesus. When he asked the villagers about their openness to the gospel, an old woman shuffled forward, bowed, and grasped Seng's hands as she said, "We have been waiting for you for twenty years." And then she told him the story of the mysterious God who had hung on the cross.

In the 1970s the Khmer Rouge, the brutal, Communist-led regime, took over Cambodia, destroying everything in its path. When the soldiers finally descended on this rural, northern village in 1979, they immediately rounded up the villagers and forced them to start digging their own graves. After the villagers had finished digging, they prepared themselves to die. Some screamed to Buddha, others screamed to demon spirits or to their ancestors.

---

[22] DORIS I. ROSSER & ELLEN VAUGHN, *The God Who Hung on the Cross* (ZONDERVAN, 2003), PP. 35-37

One of the women started to cry for help based on a childhood memory—a story her mother told her about a God who had hung on a cross. The woman prayed to that unknown God on a cross. Surely, if this God had known suffering, he would have compassion on their plight.

Suddenly, her solitary cry became one great wail as the entire village started praying to the God who had suffered and hung on a cross. As they continued facing their own graves, the wailing slowly turned to a quiet crying. There was an eerie silence in the muggy jungle air. Slowly, as they dared to turn around and face their captors, they discovered that the soldiers were gone.

As the old woman finished telling this story, she told Pastor Seng that ever since that humid day from 20 years ago the villagers had been waiting, waiting for someone to come and share the rest of the story about the God who had hung on a cross.

1. HIS FACE WAS MARRED

And some began to spit on him, and to cover his face, and to buffet him, and to say unto him, Prophesy: and the servants did strike him with the palms of their hands. – Mark 14:65

2. HIS BACK WAS MUTILATED

And so Pilate, willing to content the people, released Barabbas unto them, and delivered Jesus, when he had scourged him, to be crucified. – Mark 15:15

3. HIS BROW WAS SCARRED

And when they had platted a crown of thorns, they put it upon his head, and a reed in his right hand: and they bowed the knee before him, and mocked him, saying, Hail, King of the Jews! – Matt. 27:29

4. HIS HANDS AND FEET WERE NAILED

For dogs have compassed me: the assembly of the wicked have inclosed me: they pierced my hands and my feet. – Psalms 22:16

Behold my hands and my feet, that it is I myself: handle me, and see; for a spirit hath not flesh and bones, as ye see me have. – Luke 24:39

5. HIS SIDE WAS PIERCED

But one of the soldiers with a spear pierced his side, and forthwith came there out blood and water. – John 19:34

HE DID IT ALL FOR YOU!

23. JESUS DECLARED THE SON OF GOD

And declared to be the Son of God with power, according to the spirit of holiness, by the resurrection from the dead. – Romans 1:4

ILLUSTRATION:

[23]Pastor Clifford S. Stewart of Louisville, Kentucky, sent his parents a microwave oven one Christmas. Here's how he recalls the experience:

"They were excited that now they, too, could be a part of the instant generation. When Dad unpacked the microwave and plugged it in, literally within seconds, the microwave transformed two smiles into frowns! Even after reading the directions, they couldn't make it work. Two days later, my mother was playing bridge with a friend and confessed her inability to get that microwave oven even to boil water. 'To get this darn thing to work,' she exclaimed, 'I really don't need better directions; I just needed my son to come along with the gift!' "

When God gave the gift of salvation, he didn't send a booklet of complicated instructions for us to figure out; he sent his Son.

1. BY PROPHECY

For the prophecy came not in old time by the will of man: but holy men of God spake as they were moved by the Holy Ghost. – 2 Peter 1:21

---

[23] LEADERSHIP, VOL. 10, NO. 4

For unto us a child is born, unto us a son is given: and the government shall be upon his shoulder: and his name shall be called Wonderful, Counsellor, The mighty God, The everlasting Father, The Prince of Peace. – Isaiah 9:6

I will raise them up a Prophet from among their brethren, like unto thee, and will put my words in his mouth; and he shall speak unto them all that I shall command him. – Deut. 18:18

And I will bless them that bless thee, and curse him that curseth thee: and in thee shall all families of the earth be blessed. – Gen. 12:3

2. BY HIS LIFE

Then was Jesus led up of the Spirit into the wilderness to be tempted of the devil. And when he had fasted forty days and forty nights, he was afterward an hungred. And when the tempter came to him, he said, If thou be the Son of God, command that these stones be made bread. But he answered and said, It is written, Man shall not live by bread alone, but by every word that proceedeth out of the mouth of God. Then the devil taketh him up into the holy city, and setteth him on a pinnacle of the temple, And saith unto him, If thou be the Son of God, cast thyself down: for it is written, He shall give his angels charge concerning thee: and in their hands they shall bear thee up, lest at any time thou dash thy foot against a stone. Jesus said unto him, It is written again, Thou shalt not tempt the Lord thy God. Again, the devil taketh him up into an exceeding high mountain, and sheweth him all the kingdoms of the world, and the glory of them; And saith unto him, All these things will I give thee, if thou wilt fall down and worship me. Then saith Jesus unto him, Get thee hence, Satan: for it is written, Thou shalt worship the Lord thy God, and him only shalt thou serve. – Matt. 4:1-10

For in that he himself hath suffered being tempted, he is able to succour them that are tempted. – Heb. 2:18

For we have not an high priest which cannot be touched with the feeling of our infirmities; but was in all points tempted like as we are, yet without sin. – Heb. 4:15

And Jesus came and spake unto them, saying, All power is given unto me in heaven and in earth. – Matt. 28:18

3. BY HIS POWER

And when he thus had spoken, he cried with a loud voice, Lazarus, come forth. And he that was dead came forth, bound hand and foot with graveclothes: and his face was bound about with a napkin. Jesus saith unto them, Loose him, and let him go. – John 11:43-44

What shall we say then? Shall we continue in sin, that grace may abound? God forbid. How shall we, that are dead to sin, live any longer therein? Know ye not, that so many of us as were baptized into Jesus Christ were baptized into his death? Therefore we are buried with him by baptism into death: that like as Christ was raised up from the dead by the glory of the Father, even so we also should walk in newness of life. – Romans 6:1-4

4. BY HIS FATHER

And lo a voice from heaven, saying, This is my beloved Son, in whom I am well pleased. – Matt. 3:17

While he yet spake, behold, a bright cloud overshadowed them: and behold a voice out of the cloud, which said, This is my beloved Son, in whom I am well pleased; hear ye him. – Matt. 17:5

24. JESUS' HOUR HAD COME

These words spake Jesus, and lifted up his eyes to heaven, and said, Father, the hour is come; glorify thy Son, that thy Son also may glorify thee. – John 17:1

ILLUSTRATION:

[24]It's amazing what a difference the little things will make. For example, years ago when I was a new believer, I always wore a tiny cross pin on my shirts. Because they were an inexpensive way to witness, I'd purchase a dozen or so at a time. Every time someone commented on mine, I'd give it to them as a gift. Once in a 7-11 convenience store, the female clerk complimented my cross pin. Instinctively I offered it to her. For several moments she tried to refuse, finally reluctantly accepting the small gift.

Years went by, and I'd almost forgotten about the 7-11 woman. After church one week, a woman stopped me in the lobby and said she had to thank me. Trembling as she spoke, she explained, "You probably don't remember me, but years ago you gave me this." She reached into her purse and pulled out the small cross pin. "When you offered me this cross, my life couldn't have been any worse. I didn't feel worthy of such a generous gift. But God showed me that he still loved me. My life is different today because of what you did for me."

What I did was almost nothing. But to someone else it meant almost everything.

---

[24] CRAIG GROESCHEL, THE CHRISTIAN ATHEIST (ZONDERVAN, 2011). P. 210

1. IT WAS THE DESTINED HOUR

But with the precious blood of Christ, as of a lamb without blemish and without spot: Who verily was foreordained before the foundation of the world, but was manifest in these last times for you. – 1 Peter 1:19-20

2. IT WAS THE DETERMINED HOUR

Know therefore and understand, that from the going forth of the commandment to restore and to build Jerusalem unto the Messiah the Prince shall be seven weeks, and threescore and two weeks: the street shall be built again, and the wall, even in troublous times. And after threescore and two weeks shall Messiah be cut off, but not for himself: and the people of the prince that shall come shall destroy the city and the sanctuary; and the end thereof shall be with a flood, and unto the end of the war desolations are determined. – Dan. 9:25-26

3. IT WAS THE DEFINED HOUR

For then must he often have suffered since the foundation of the world: but now once in the end of the world hath he appeared to put away sin by the sacrifice of himself. – Heb. 9:26

4. IT WAS THE DEMONSTRATED HOUR

But God commendeth his love toward us, in that, while we were yet sinners, Christ died for us. Much more then, being now justified by his blood, we shall be saved from wrath through him. – Romans 5:8-9

5. IT WAS THE DISTINGUISHED HOUR

And Jesus answered them, saying, The hour is come, that the Son of man should be glorified. – John 12:23

25. WHAT DID JESUS TEACH? – PART 1

ILLUSTRATION:
[25]An item in "The Report Card" told of a study done in Colorado in which 3000 high school seniors were asked about their best teachers. From their responses this composite was drawn. The ideal teacher (1) is genuinely concerned and interested in students as individuals; (2) requires students to work; (3) is impartial in dealing with students; and (4) is obviously enthusiastic about teaching.

1. THE NEED FOR THE NEW BIRTH

Jesus answered and said unto him, Verily, verily, I say unto thee, Except a man be born again, he cannot see the kingdom of God. – John 3:3

2. THE NECESSITY OF HIS DEATH

And as Moses lifted up the serpent in the wilderness, even so must the Son of man be lifted up. – John 3:14

3. THE LOVE OF GOD THROUGH THE GIFT OF HIS SON

---

[25] *Today In The Word*, Oct, 1989, p. 25.

For God so loved the world, that he gave his only begotten Son, that whosoever believeth in him should not perish, but have everlasting life. – John 3:16

4. THE PREVALENCE OF EVIL

And this is the condemnation, that light is come into the world, and men loved darkness rather than light, because their deeds were evil. – John 3:19

5. THE POSSESSION OF ETERNAL LIFE

He that believeth on the Son hath everlasting life: and he that believeth not the Son shall not see life; but the wrath of God abideth on him. – John 3:36

26. WHAT DID JESUS TEACH? – PART 2

ILLUSTRATION:

[26]Life is a matter of building. Each of us has the opportunity to build something -- a secure family, a good reputation, a career, a relationship to God. But some of those things can disappear almost overnight due to financial losses, natural disasters and other unforeseen difficulties.

What are we to do? Daniel Webster offered excellent advice, saying, "If we work on marble it will perish. If we work on brass, time will efface it. If we rear temples, they will crumble to dust. But if we work on men's immortal minds, if we imbue them with high principles, with just fear of God and love of their fellow-men, we engrave on those tablets something which time cannot efface, and which will brighten and brighten to all eternity.

There is no better way to that than to learn from the Master Teacher, Jesus.

1. THE WAY OF DISCIPLESHIP

Then said Jesus to those Jews which believed on him, If ye continue in my word, then are ye my disciples indeed. – John 8:31

---

[26] *Morning Glory*, July 3, 1993.

2. THE FREEDOM GIVING POWER OF TRUTH

And ye shall know the truth, and the truth shall make you free. – John 8:32

3. THE HOME THAT AWAITS BELIEVERS

Let not your heart be troubled: ye believe in God, believe also in me. In my Father's house are many mansions: if it were not so, I would have told you. I go to prepare a place for you. And if I go and prepare a place for you, I will come again, and receive you unto myself; that where I am, there ye may be also. – John 14:1-3

4. THE NECESSITY OF FRUIT-BEARING

I am the vine, ye are the branches: He that abideth in me, and I in him, the same bringeth forth much fruit: for without me ye can do nothing. – John 15:5

5. THE TRUTH OF GOD'S WORD

Sanctify them through thy truth: thy word is truth. – John 17:17

27. JESUS WAS DIFFERENT

ILLUSTRATION:
[27]C.S. Lewis said, "I am trying here to prevent anyone saying the really foolish thing that people often say about him: "I'm ready to accept Jesus as a great moral teacher, but I don't accept his claim to be God." That is the one thing we must not say. A man who was merely a man and said the sort of things Jesus said would not be a great moral teacher. He would either be a lunatic—on a level with the man who says he is a poached egg—or else he would be the Devil of hell. You must make your choice. Either this man was, and is, the Son of God: or else a madman or something worse. You can shut him up for a fool, you can spit at him and kill him as a demon; or you can fall at his feet and call him Lord and God. But let us not come with any patronizing nonsense about his being a great human teacher. He has not left that open to us. He did not intend to."

1. JESUS HAD A DIFFERENT KIND OF BIRTH

Therefore the Lord himself shall give you a sign; Behold, a virgin shall conceive, and bear a son, and shall call his name Immanuel. – Isaiah 7:14

2. JESUS HAD A DIFFERENT KIND OF LIFE

---

[27] C.S. LEWIS, MERE CHRISTIANITY

For we have not an high priest which cannot be touched with the feeling of our infirmities; but was in all points tempted like as we are, yet without sin. – Heb. 4:15

3. JESUS HAD A DIFFERENT KIND OF AUTHORITY

And Jesus came and spake unto them, saying, All power is given unto me in heaven and in earth. – Matt. 28:18

4. JESUS HAD A DIFFERENT KIND OF DEATH

And for this cause he is the mediator of the new testament, that by means of death, for the redemption of the transgressions that were under the first testament, they which are called might receive the promise of eternal inheritance. – Heb. 9:15

5. JESUS HAD A DIFFERENT KIND OF KINGDOM

Jesus answered, My kingdom is not of this world: if my kingdom were of this world, then would my servants fight, that I should not be delivered to the Jews: but now is my kingdom not from hence. – John 18:36

28. WHAT GOOD DID JESUS DO?

God anointed Jesus of Nazareth with the Holy Ghost and with power: <u>who went about doing good</u>, and healing all that were oppressed of the devil; for God was with him. – Acts 10:38

ILLUSTRATION:

[28]My 5-year-old, Carl, and my 3-year-old, Conrad, love it when I dress like them. After they put on jeans and a blue T-shirt, they'll come ask me to wear jeans and a blue T-shirt. When I do, they have a saying. They will survey me, survey themselves, and say, "Look, Dad—same, same." For my birthday, Carl bought me a North Carolina blue mesh shirt ... because he has a North Carolina blue mesh shirt. We could be "same, same."

When I play living room football with my boys, Conrad will not let me play standing—so big and scary and towering above him. The theological term for this is "completely Other." Instead he insists I get on my knees. When I am down at eye-level, Conrad puts his hand on my shoulder and says, "There. See, Dad—same, same." They like it when I enter their world ....

---

[28] MATT PROCTOR, "CAROLS FOR ANY SEASON OF SUFFERING," *Christian Standard* MAGAZINE (12-23-07)

This summer, I scraped my leg working on my house. When Conrad fell down and scraped his leg, he pointed at my scab, then showed me his and said, "Hey, Dad—same, same."

Here's the point … God himself has felt what we feel. In the Incarnation, he chose not to stay "completely Other." He got down at eye-level, and in the Incarnation, God experienced what it's like to be tired and discouraged …. He knows what it's like to hurt and bleed. On the cross, Jesus himself prayed a psalm of lament: "My God, my God, why have you forsaken me?" (Psalm 22:1).

In your pain, you may be tempted to say, "God, you have no idea what I'm going through. You have no idea how bad I'm hurting." But God can respond, "Yes, I do." He can point to your wounds and then to his own and say, "Look: same, same. Me too. I have entered your world, and I know how you feel. I have been there, I am with you now, I care, and I can help."

1. JESUS WENT ABOUT HIS FATHER'S BUSINESS

And he said unto them, How is it that ye sought me? wist ye not that I must be about my Father's business? And they understood not the saying which he spake unto them.

And he went down with them, and came to Nazareth, and was subject unto them: but his mother kept all these sayings in her heart. And Jesus increased in wisdom and stature, and in favour with God and man. – Luke 2:49-52

2. JESUS HEALED THE SICK

And Jesus went about all Galilee, teaching in their synagogues, and preaching the gospel of the kingdom, and healing all manner of sickness and all manner of disease among the people. And his fame went throughout all Syria: and they brought unto him all sick people that were taken with divers diseases and torments, and those which were possessed with devils, and those which were lunatick, and those that had the palsy; and he healed them. – Matt. 4:23-24

3. JESUS RETURNED GOOD FOR EVIL

But I say unto you, Love your enemies, bless them that curse you, do good to them that hate you, and pray for them which despitefully use you, and persecute you. – Matt. 5:44

4. JESUS WAS A FRIEND TO THE FRIENDLESS

And when the Pharisees saw it, they said unto his disciples, Why eateth your Master with publicans and sinners? But when Jesus heard that, he said unto them, They that be whole need not a physician, but they that are sick. – Matt. 9:11-12

5. JESUS LEFT AN EXAMPLE FOR US TO FOLLOW

For even hereunto were ye called: because Christ also suffered for us, leaving us an example, that ye should follow his steps. – 1 Peter 2:21

29. WHEN JESUS LOOKS AT YOU

ILLUSTRATION:

[29]To explain how God sees human sinfulness, Billy Graham writes:

Cliff Barrows and I were in Atlantic City many years ago with our wives. We had had a service, and we were walking down the boardwalk. A man was auctioning diamonds and other jewelry. We decided to go in. When we got married, I had given my wife a diamond that was so small, you couldn't see it with a microscope. So I decided to get her a better diamond. I had $65 in my pocket. I eventually bid it all and bought the diamond. It was a perfect diamond, I thought. The next day, I went to a jeweler, and I said, "Can you look at this diamond and tell me how much it is worth?"

He looked at it through his glass and said, "Oh, maybe $35 or $40."

"What?" I said. "This is supposed to be two carats!"

"Look at it," he said and gave the glass to me. I looked at it, and even I could see it was full of defects.

---

[29] BILLY GRAHAM, "THE MEANING OF THE CROSS," DECISION (JANUARY 2005)

And that's the way God looks at us. We go to church and pray. We are good, moral people. But he looks at us through his own righteousness, and he sees in all of us the defects of our sin.

1. HE SEES WHAT YOU ARE AND STILL LOVES YOU

For all have sinned, and come short of the glory of God. – Romans 3:23

2. HE SEES WHAT YOU HAVE DONE AND WANTS TO CHANGE YOU

Come, see a man, which told me all things that ever I did: is not this the Christ? – John 4:29

3. HE SEES WHAT YOU NEED AND OFFERS IT TO YOU

Jesus answered, Verily, verily, I say unto thee, Except a man be born of water and of the Spirit, he cannot enter into the kingdom of God. That which is born of the flesh is flesh; and that which is born of the Spirit is spirit. Marvel not that I said unto thee, Ye must be born again. – John 3:5-7

4. HE SEES WHAT YOU WANT AND GIVES IT TO YOU

Then Simon Peter answered him, Lord, to whom shall we go? thou hast the words of eternal life. – John 6:68

My sheep hear my voice, and I know them, and they follow me: And I give unto them eternal life; and they shall never perish, neither shall any man pluck them out of my hand. My Father, which gave them me, is greater than all; and no man is able to pluck them out of my Father's hand. I and my Father are one. – John 10:27-30

5. HE SEES YOUR TRIALS AND REASSURES YOU

Wherein ye greatly rejoice, though now for a season, if need be, ye are in heaviness through manifold temptations: That the trial of your faith, being much more precious than of gold that perisheth, though it be tried with fire, might be found unto praise and honour and glory at the appearing of Jesus Christ. – 1 Peter 1:6-7

30. WHEN YOU LOOK AT JESUS...

ILLUSTRATION:

[30]Imagine the mystery and delight of not just hearing, but seeing the story of Jesus for the first time, almost as an eyewitness.

That's what happened to a tribe in the jungles of East Asia when missionaries showed them the Jesus film. Not only had these people never heard of Jesus, they had never seen a motion picture. Then, on one unforgettable evening, they saw it all—the gospel in their own language, visible and real.

Imagine again how it felt to see this good man, Jesus, who healed the sick and was adored by children, held without trial and beaten by jeering soldiers. As they watched this, the people came unglued. They stood up and began to shout at the cruel men on the screen, demanding that this outrage stop.

When nothing happened, they attacked the missionary running the projector. Perhaps he was responsible for this injustice! He was forced to stop the film and explain that the story wasn't over yet,; there was more. So they settled back onto the ground, holding their emotions in tenuous check.

Then came the crucifixion. Again, the people could not hold back. They began to weep and wail with such loud grief that, once again, the film had to be stopped. The

---

[30] BEN PATTERSON, "RESURRECTION AND PANDEMONIUM," LEADERSHIPJOURNAL.NET 4-13-04

missionary again tried to calm them, explaining that the story still wasn't over; there was more. So they composed themselves and sat down to see what happened next.

Then came the resurrection. Pandemonium broke out this time, but for a different reason. The gathering had spontaneously erupted into a party. The noise now was of jubilation, and it was deafening. The people were dancing and slapping each other on the back. Christ is risen, indeed!

Again the missionary had to shut off the projector; this time he didn't tell them to calm down and wait for what was next. All that was supposed to happen—in the story and in their lives—was happening.

1. DO YOU SEE HIM WITH THE EYE OF FAITH?

And the apostles said unto the Lord, Increase our faith. – Luke 17:5

2. DO YOU SEE HIM WITH THE EYE OF LOVE?

And said, Behold, I see the heavens opened, and the Son of man standing on the right hand of God. – Acts 7:56

3. DO YOU SEE HIM WITH THE EYE OF RECOGNITION?

Jesus saith unto her, Mary. She turned herself, and saith unto him, Rabboni; which is to say, Master. – John 20:16

4. DO YOU SEE HIM WITH THE EYE OF UNDERSTANDING?

Wherefore seeing we also are compassed about with so great a cloud of witnesses, let us lay aside every weight, and the sin which doth so easily beset us, and let us run with patience the race that is set before us, Looking unto Jesus the author and finisher of our faith; who for the joy that was set before him endured the cross, despising the shame, and is set down at the right hand of the throne of God. – Heb. 12:1-2

5. DO YOU SEE HIM WITH THE EYE OF REALITY?

And when he had so said, he shewed unto them his hands and his side. Then were the disciples glad, when they saw the Lord. – John 20:20

6. DO YOU SEE HIM WITH THE EYE OF HOPE?

Looking for that blessed hope, and the glorious appearing of the great God and our Saviour Jesus Christ. – Titus 2:13

31. HOW TO WALK LIKE JESUS

That ye might walk worthy of the Lord unto all pleasing, being fruitful in every good work, and increasing in the knowledge of God. – Col. 1:10

ILLUSTRATION:

[31]It was six o'clock in the morning, and I had just finished my early run. As I passed the local Starbucks, I decided to stop in and get a couple cups of our favorite lattes and take them home to [my wife], who would be waking up. Since the café had just opened, there was only one other person in line in front of me. But it wasn't your ordinary wait-in-line-for-coffee drill. The guy in front of me was in a tense argument with the clerk. In loud and no uncertain terms, the customer was complaining that all he wanted was the copy of the NEW YORK TIMES that he was holding in one hand while he was waving a fifty-dollar bill in the other. The fight was over the fact that the clerk did not have enough change yet to break the fifty-dollar bill, which made it impossible for him to sell the paper.

It dawned on me that this was an early morning opportunity to commit one intentional act of [goodness] by demonstrating the excellence of the generous spirit of Jesus. So I said to the clerk, "Hey, put the paper on my bill; I'll buy it for him." This immediately defused the tension, and the grateful New York Times guy walked away saying, "Thanks a lot. All I have is yours!" Which evidently did not include the fifty-dollar bill.

---

[31] JOE STOWELL, *Jesus Nation* (TYNDALE, 2009), PP. 80-81

To my surprise, when the barista handed me my coffee, he said, "Mister, that was a really nice thing for you to do. This world would be a lot better place to live if more people were like you." What he didn't know was that if he really knew me, he probably wouldn't say that.

His comments caught me totally off guard, and I knew that I could say something at that point that would point the glory upward...but nothing came. So I made some self-deprecating remark and walked out, haunted that I had missed a great opportunity to glorify God. As I was walking down the sidewalk, it came to me. I should have said, "Well, this world would not be a better place if more people were like me. But it would be a better place if more people were like Jesus, because he taught me how to do that."

I turned around to go back and tell him that, only to remember that by the time I left there was a line waiting for coffee. It didn't seem to me that it would be a great idea to break into the line and make a religious speech. My only conclusion was the thought that I was wearing my Moody Bible Institute hat. So I prayed that he would have noticed my hat. That he would always remember that Bible people do things like that, and that the world would be a better place if there were more Bible people around.

1. WALK BY FAITH

For we walk by faith, not by sight. – 2 Cor. 5:7

2. WALK IN THE SPIRIT

This I say then, Walk in the Spirit, and ye shall not fulfil the lust of the flesh. – Gal. 5:16

3. WALK IN LOVE

And walk in love, as Christ also hath loved us, and hath given himself for us an offering and a sacrifice to God for a sweetsmelling savour. – Eph. 5:2

4. WALK IN WISDOM

Walk in wisdom toward them that are without, redeeming the time. – Col. 4:5

5. WALK IN THE TRUTH

I have no greater joy than to hear that my children walk in truth. – 3 John 4

6. WALK AFTER HIS COMMANDMENTS

And this is love, that we walk after his commandments. This is the commandment, That, as ye have heard from the beginning, ye should walk in it. – 2 John 6

32. JESUS WAS ABOUT HIS FATHER'S BUSINESS

And he said unto them, How is it that ye sought me? wist ye not that I must be about my Father's business? – Luke 2:49

ILLUSTRATION:

[32]In his book THOUGHTS IN SOLITUDE, Thomas Merton wrote fifteen lines that have become known as "the Merton Prayer":

My Lord God, I have no idea where I am going. I do not see the road ahead of me. I cannot know for certain where it will end. Nor do I really know myself, and the fact that I think I am following your will does not mean that I am actually doing so. But I believe that the desire to please you does in fact please you. And I hope I have that desire in all that I am doing. I hope that I will never do anything apart from that desire. And I know that if I do this you will lead me by the right road, though I may know nothing about it. Therefore I will trust you always though I may seem to be lost and in the shadow of death. I will not fear, for you are ever with me, and you will never leave me to face my perils alone.

1. DOING THE FATHER'S WORK

---

[32] THOMAS MERTON, *Thoughts in Solitude* (FARRAR, STRAUS AND GIROUX, 1999), P. 79

If I do not the works of my Father, believe me not. – John 10:37

2. PROCLAIMING THE FATHER'S WORDS

For I have given unto them the words which thou gavest me; and they have received them, and have known surely that I came out from thee, and they have believed that thou didst send me. – John 17:8

3. REVEALING THE FATHER'S CHARACTER

No man hath seen God at any time; the only begotten Son, which is in the bosom of the Father, he hath declared him. – John 1:18

4. CARRYING ON THE FATHER'S WILL

Saying, Father, if thou be willing, remove this cup from me: nevertheless not my will, but thine, be done. – Luke 22:42

5. GLORIFYING THE FATHER'S NAME

Father, glorify thy name. Then came there a voice from heaven, saying, I have both glorified it, and will glorify it again. – John 12:28

6. BRINGING TO THE FATHER'S HOUSE

In my Father's house are many mansions: if it were not so, I would have told you. I go to prepare a place for you. – John 14:2

7. UNFOLDING THE FATHER'S LOVE

For the Father himself loveth you, because ye have loved me, and have believed that I came out from God. – John 16:27

33. JESUS DID IT FOR US

ILLUSTRATION:

[33]In August 1957 four climbers—two Italians and two Germans—were climbing the 6,000 foot near-vertical North Face in the Swiss Alps. The two German climbers disappeared and were never heard from again. The two Italian climbers, exhausted and dying, were stuck on two narrow ledges a thousand feet below the summit. The Swiss Alpine Club forbade rescue attempts in this area (it was just too dangerous), but a small group of Swiss climbers decided to launch a private rescue effort to save the Italians. So they carefully lowered a climber named Alfred Hellepart down the 6,000 foot North Face. They suspended Hellepart on a cable a fraction of an inch thick as they lowered him into the abyss.

Here's how Hellepart described the rescue in his own words:

As I was lowered down the summit … my comrades on top grew further and further distant, until they disappeared from sight. At this moment I felt an indescribable aloneness. Then for the first time I peered down the abyss of the North Face of the Eiger. The terror of the sight robbed me of breath. …The brooding blackness of the Face, falling away in almost endless expanse beneath me, made me look with awful longing to the thin cable disappearing about me in the mist. I was a tiny human being

---

[33] JAMES R. EDWARDS, *Is Jesus the Only Savior* (WILLIAM B. EERDMANS PUBLISHING COMPANY, 2005), PP. 160-161

dangling in space between heaven and hell. The sole relief from terror was …my mission to save the climber below.

That is the heart of the Gospel story. We were trapped, but in the person and presence of Jesus, God lowered himself into the abyss of our sin and suffering. In Jesus God became "a tiny human being dangling between heaven and hell." He did it to save the people trapped below—you and me. Thus, the gospel is much more radical than just another religion telling us how to be good in our own power. It tells us the story of God's risky, costly, sacrificial rescue effort on our behalf.

1. BECAME POOR SO WE MIGHT BECOME RICH

Hearken, my beloved brethren, Hath not God chosen the poor of this world rich in faith, and heirs of the kingdom which he hath promised to them that love him? – James 2:5

2. JESUS WAS BORN SO WE MIGHT BE BORN AGAIN

And the Word was made flesh, and dwelt among us, (and we beheld his glory, the glory as of the only begotten of the Father,) full of grace and truth. – John 1:14

3. JESUS BECAME A SERVANT SO WE MIGHT BECOME SONS

But when the fulness of the time was come, God sent forth his Son, made of a woman, made under the law, To redeem them that were under the law, that we might receive the adoption of sons. And because ye are sons, God hath sent forth the Spirit of his Son into your hearts, crying, Abba, Father. – Gal. 4:4-6

4. JESUSHAD NO HOME SO WE MIGHT HAVE AN ETERNAL HOME

And Jesus saith unto him, The foxes have holes, and the birds of the air have nests; but the Son of man hath not where to lay his head. – Matt. 8:20

5. JESUS WAS BOUND SO WE MIGHT GO FREE

And ye shall know the truth, and the truth shall make you free. They answered him, We be Abraham's seed, and were never in bondage to any man: how sayest thou, Ye shall be made free? Jesus answered them, Verily, verily, I say unto you, Whosoever committeth sin is the servant of sin. And the servant abideth not in the house for ever: but the Son abideth ever. If the Son therefore shall make you free, ye shall be free indeed. I know that ye are Abraham's seed; but ye seek to kill me, because my word hath no place in you. – John 8:32-37

6. JESUS WAS MADE SIN SO WE MIGHT BE MADE RIGHTEOUS

For he hath made him to be sin for us, who knew no sin; that we might be made the righteousness of God in him. – 2 Cor. 5:21

7. JESUS DIED SO WE MIGHT LIVE

For God hath not appointed us to wrath, but to obtain salvation by our Lord Jesus Christ, Who died for us, that, whether we wake or sleep, we should live together with him. – 1 Thess. 5:9-10

34. JESUS' CALL TO SALVATION

ILLUSTRATION:

[34]On a cold winter day Gabriel Estrada, a high school senior in Twin Lakes, Wisconsin, did the unthinkable. When his 17-year-old girlfriend secretly gave birth to a baby boy on January 15, 2002, she dressed it and asked him to deliver it to a church. Instead, Gabriel wrapped the baby in a canvas bag and left him in a portable toilet in a nearby park to die. But against incredible odds the baby was saved.

According to police there was virtually no chance the infant would survive. Temperatures were well below freezing. Lack of snow meant the nearby sledding hill would not be frequented by kids. And the sanitation company's scheduled pick-up at the port-a-potty was days away.

Village of Twin Lakes police credit a father and son for saving the child's life. About 4 o'clock in the afternoon on January 16th a father (wishing to remain anonymous) and his young son stopped at the abandoned West Side Park in need of a bathroom. Hearing a whimpering sound coming from the port-a-potty, they knew something was wrong. They called 911 to report what they had discovered.

When Officer Randy Prudik responded to the call, he pulled the canvas bag from the outdoor toilet and raced to nearby Burlington Memorial Hospital where the baby received emergency treatment.

---

[34] MILWAUKEE JOURNAL SENTINEL (1-7-02)

"There's no way he would have survived that," Prudik said. "That little guy had somebody watching over him."

As a testament to the boy's survival, the nurses at the hospital dubbed him William Grant: William for the will to live and Grant for not taking life for granted.

On a grander scale, another Father and Son rescue team intervened on behalf of doomed humanity. "For God so loved the world that he gave his only son that whosoever believes in him would not perish but have eternal life" (John 3:16).

1. JESUS CALLS US TO HEAR

Verily, verily, I say unto you, He that heareth my word, and believeth on him that sent me, hath everlasting life, and shall not come into condemnation; but is passed from death unto life. – John 5:24

2. JESUS CALLS US TO BELIEVE

And he said unto them, Ye are from beneath; I am from above: ye are of this world; I am not of this world. I said therefore unto you, that ye shall die in your sins: for if ye believe not that I am he, ye shall die in your sins. – John 8:23-24

3. JESUS CALLS US TO REPENT

I tell you, Nay: but, except ye repent, ye shall all likewise perish. – Luke 13:3

4. JESUS CALLS US TO CONFESS HIM

Whosoever therefore shall confess me before men, him will I confess also before my Father which is in heaven. – Matt. 10:32

5. JESUS CALLS US TO BE BAPTIZED

He that believeth and is baptized shall be saved; but he that believeth not shall be damned. – Mark 16:16

35. WHAT JESUS' CROSS DID TO SIN

ILLUSTRATION:

[35]Theologian Alister McGrath outlines the following three stages of receiving what Christ did for us on the cross:

[First], I may believe that God is promising me forgiveness of sins; [second], I may trust that promise; but [third] unless I respond to that promise, I shall not obtain forgiveness. The first two stages of faith prepare the way for the third, without it they are incomplete.

Then he illustrates these three stages with the following true story:

Consider a bottle of penicillin, the famous antibiotic identified by Alexander Fleming, and first produced for clinical use in [Great Britain]. The drug was responsible for saving the lives of countless individuals who would otherwise have died from various forms of blood poisoning. Think of the three stages of faith like this. I may ACCEPT that the bottle exists. I may TRUST in its ability to cure blood poisoning. But nothing will change unless I RECEIVE the drug which it contains. I must allow it to destroy the bacteria which are slowly killing me. Otherwise, I have not benefited from my faith in it.

---

[35] ALISTER E. MCGRATH, *What Was God Doing on the Cross* (ZONDERVAN, 1992), PP. 99-100

It is the third element of faith which is of vital importance in making sense of the cross. Just as faith links a bottle of penicillin to the cure of blood poisoning, so faith forges a link between the cross and resurrection of Jesus Christ and ourselves. Faith unites us with the risen Christ, and makes available to us everything he gained through his obedience and resurrection.

1. THE CROSS REMOVED SIN'S HINDRANCE

For then must he often have suffered since the foundation of the world: but now once in the end of the world hath he appeared to put away sin by the sacrifice of himself. – Heb. 9:26

2. THE CROSS ANSWERS FOR SIN'S GUILT

Who his own self bare our sins in his own body on the tree, that we, being dead to sins, should live unto righteousness: by whose stripes ye were healed. – 1 Peter 2:24

3. THE CROSS OVERTHREW SIN'S AUTHOR

Forasmuch then as the children are partakers of flesh and blood, he also himself likewise took part of the same; that through death he might destroy him that had the power of death, that is, the devil. – Heb. 2:14

4. THE CROSS SPANNED SIN'S GULF

Having therefore, brethren, boldness to enter into the holiest by the blood of Jesus, By a new and living way, which he hath consecrated for us, through the veil, that is to say, his flesh. – Heb. 10:19-20

5. THE CROSS REMOVED SIN'S POLLUTION

By the which will we are sanctified through the offering of the body of Jesus Christ once for all. – Heb. 10:10

6. THE CROSS BROKE SIN'S POWER

This is the covenant that I will make with them after those days, saith the Lord, I will put my laws into their hearts, and in their minds will I write them; And their sins and iniquities will I remember no more. Now where remission of these is, there is no more offering for sin. – Heb. 10:16-18

7. THE CROSS DESTROYED SIN'S VICTORY

He that committeth sin is of the devil; for the devil sinneth from the beginning. For this purpose the Son of God was manifested, that he might destroy the works of the devil. – 1 John 3:8

36. FACTS ABOUT CHRIST'S DEATH

ILLUSTRATION:

[36]The Old Testament word for worm is TOLA'ATH. This little worm from the Middle East is something like the cochineal of Mexico. When these creatures are crushed, the blood makes a brilliant crimson dye used in the bright Mexican garments. In Palestine and Syria, the TOLA'ATH similarly makes a beautiful permanent scarlet dye. It is very expensive and worn by the rich and noble. In a sense, the word SCARLET means "the splendor of the worm."

Saul is said to have clothed the maidens of Israel in scarlet (2 Samuel 1:24). Belshazzar promised Daniel scarlet clothing as a reward (Daniel 5:16). The scarlet producing worm is even used in a text prophetic of the Messiah. "I am a worm (tola'ath), and no man" (Psalm 22:6).

The glorious garments of our salvation have been procured as a result of Christ's death and suffering. He became the TOLA'ATH – crushed in death – so that we may be robed in glory.

1. IT WAS UNJUSTIFIED IN CAUSE

Him, being delivered by the determinate counsel and foreknowledge of God, ye have taken, and by wicked hands have crucified and slain. – Acts 2:23

2. IT WAS UNIQUE IN FULFILLMENT

---

[36] INTERNATIONAL STANDARD BIBLE ENCYCLOPEDIA

That the saying of Jesus might be fulfilled, which he spake, signifying what death he should die. – John 18:32

3. IT WAS UNPARALLELED IN EXPERIENCE

But we see Jesus, who was made a little lower than the angels for the suffering of death, crowned with glory and honour; that he by the grace of God should taste death for every man. – Heb. 2:9

4. IT WAS SUBSTITUTIONARY IN FACT

For Christ also hath once suffered for sins, the just for the unjust, that he might bring us to God, being put to death in the flesh, but quickened by the Spirit. – 1 Peter 3:18

5. IT WAS RECONCILING IN EFFECT

For if, when we were enemies, we were reconciled to God by the death of his Son, much more, being reconciled, we shall be saved by his life. – Romans 5:10

6. IT WAS SEPARATING IN INFLUENCE

Likewise reckon ye also yourselves to be dead indeed unto sin, but alive unto God through Jesus Christ our Lord. – Romans 6:11

7. IT WAS CONFORMING IN POWER

That I may know him, and the power of his resurrection, and the fellowship of his sufferings, being made conformable unto his death. – Phil. 3:10

37. THE "I AMS" OF JESUS – PART 1

ILLUSTRATION:

[37]Author Frederica Mathewes-Green addresses people who hunger for God's presence but rarely feel it—at least not in dramatic ways. She writes:

My hunch is that you are already sensing something of God's presence, or you wouldn't care. Picture yourself walking around a shopping mall, looking at people and the window displays. Suddenly, you get a whiff of cinnamon. You weren't even hungry, but now you really crave a cinnamon roll. This craving isn't something you made up. There you were, minding your own business, when some drifting molecules of sugar, butter, and spice collided with a susceptible patch inside your nose. You had a real encounter with cinnamon—not a mental delusion, not an emotional projection, but the real thing.

And what was the effect? You want more, NOW. And if you hunger to know the presence of God, it's because ... you have already begun to scent [God's] compelling delight.

Jesus proves to us beyond any doubt in His "I Am" statements, that he is the One who can satisfy our every desire.

---

[37] FREDERICA MATHEWES-GREEN, *The Jesus Prayer* (PARACLETE PRESS, 2009), PP. XIII-XIV

1. I AM THE BREAD OF LIFE

And Jesus said unto them, I am the bread of life: he that cometh to me shall never hunger; and he that believeth on me shall never thirst. – John 6:35

2. I AM THE LIGHT OF THE WORLD

Then spake Jesus again unto them, saying, I am the light of the world: he that followeth me shall not walk in darkness, but shall have the light of life. – John 8:12

3. I AM THE DOOR OF THE SHEEP

Then said Jesus unto them again, Verily, verily, I say unto you, I am the door of the sheep. All that ever came before me are thieves and robbers: but the sheep did not hear them. I am the door: by me if any man enter in, he shall be saved, and shall go in and out, and find pasture. – John 10:7-9

4. I AM THE GOOD SHEPHERD

I am the good shepherd: the good shepherd giveth his life for the sheep. But he that is an hireling, and not the shepherd, whose own the sheep are not, seeth the wolf coming, and leaveth the sheep, and fleeth: and the wolf catcheth them, and scattereth the sheep. The hireling fleeth, because he is an hireling, and careth not for the sheep. I am the good shepherd, and know my sheep, and am known of mine. As the Father knoweth me, even so know I the Father: and I lay down my life for the sheep. – John 10:11-15

5. I AM THE RESURRECTION AND THE LIFE

Jesus said unto her, I am the resurrection, and the life: he that believeth in me, though he were dead, yet shall he live: And whosoever liveth and believeth in me shall never die. Believest thou this? – John 11:25-26

38. THE "I AMS" OF JESUS – PART 2

ILLUSTRATION:

[38]Jeremy Bowen, the presenter of a new British Broadcasting Corporation (BBC) documentary on Jesus stated, "The important thing is not what he was or what he wasn't—the important things is what people believe him to have been. A massive worldwide religion, numbering more than two billion people follows his memory—that's pretty remarkable, 2,000 years on."

Bowen couldn't be more wrong. Who Jesus is and what he did is the foundation of our faith.

1. I AM THE WAY, THE TRUTH, AND THE LIFE

Jesus saith unto him, I am the way, the truth, and the life: no man cometh unto the Father, but by me. – John 14:6

2. I AM THE TRUE VINE

I am the true vine, and my Father is the husbandman. Every branch in me that beareth not fruit he taketh away: and every branch that beareth fruit, he purgeth it, that it may bring forth more fruit. Now ye are clean through the word which I have spoken unto you. Abide in me, and I in you. As the branch cannot bear fruit of itself, except it

---

[38] ALEX WEBB, "LOOKING FOR THE HISTORICAL JESUS," BBC NEWS ONLINE,(3-26-01 COLUMN)

abide in the vine; no more can ye, except ye abide in me. I am the vine, ye are the branches: He that abideth in me, and I in him, the same bringeth forth much fruit: for without me ye can do nothing. – John 15:1-5

3. I AM THE ALPHA AND OMEGA, THE FIRST AND THE LAST

Saying, I am Alpha and Omega, the first and the last: and, What thou seest, write in a book, and send it unto the seven churches which are in Asia; unto Ephesus, and unto Smyrna, and unto Pergamos, and unto Thyatira, and unto Sardis, and unto Philadelphia, and unto Laodicea. – Rev. 1:11

4. I AM THE BRIGHT AND MORNING STAR

I Jesus have sent mine angel to testify unto you these things in the churches. I am the root and the offspring of David, and the bright and morning star. – Rev. 22:16

5. I AM HE THAT SEARCHETH THE REINS AND HEARTS

And I will kill her children with death; and all the churches shall know that I am he which searcheth the reins and hearts: and I will give unto every one of you according to your works. – Rev. 2:23

39. GETTING TO KNOW JESUS

That I may know him, and the power of his resurrection, and the fellowship of his sufferings, being made conformable unto his death. – Phil. 3:10

ILLUSTRATION:

[39]In seminary my Bible professor was Manfred George Gutzke, a Canadian like myself who had an impressively large physique and had been the boxing champion of the Canadian Army in his youth. Everything about him seemed oversized: his huge hairless head, his enormous eyebrows, his low gravelly voice, his sweeping knowledge of the Scriptures.

Not only did he hold us spellbound with his grasp of the Bible; he also fascinated us with stories of his own life. ...

Manfred Gutzke was a man of God, as well as a teacher of preachers, but he had not started out religious in any formal sense. For many years he was an agnostic. Yet in the years when he was teaching in a one-room rural school on the prairies of western Canada, he began to be a seeker, wondering whether there might be a God and he could know him.

He was especially impressed by a devout farmer who moved into that small community. This man sold two cows and donated the proceeds to missionary work on the annual missions Sunday. This was cause for amazement at the small prairie church, where most of the farmers came

---

[39] LEIGHTON FORD, *The Attentive Life* (IVP, 2008), PP. 79-80

because there was nothing better to do on a Sunday morning. Most of them stood outside and gossiped with their friends until long after the service began. But this new man arrived carrying a Bible, went straight into the church, and bowed his head in prayer.

Here was someone whose faith seemed central, and the young teacher was intrigued.

One afternoon after school, making his way across the fields to his boarding house, [Gutzke] was struck by this thought: IF GOD EXISTS, THEN HE CAN SEE ME RIGHT NOW!

"I stood in that field," he told us, "and pondered that thought. If God exists, he could see me.

"So," he said, "I took off my hat! That may seem strange, but like most men in those days I wore a brimmed hat, and I always took it off in the presence of women, older people, or other important persons. So I took my hat off to God.

"And then I prayed: 'God, I do not know whether you are there or not. And I don't mean anything bad by that. I just don't know. But I want to know, and you know that too. So please show me if you are real.'

"I felt," he said, "as if something very important had happened."

Then he put his hat back on and made his way home.

He had taken the first step toward his spiritual home that day. For the very first time, Manfred Gutzke paid attention to God—the God who was already paying attention to him. And before much more time had passed, he would come to prove in his own life the affirmation of Jesus, "Seek and you shall find," and the promise in Hebrews 11:6 of a God who "rewards those who earnestly seek him."

1. MEDITATE ON HIM AND HIS WORD

My meditation of him shall be sweet: I will be glad in the LORD. – Psalms 104:34

But his delight is in the law of the LORD; and in his law doth he meditate day and night. – Psalms 1:2

2. MAGNIFY HIM THROUGH PRAYER

But thou, when thou prayest, enter into thy closet, and when thou hast shut thy door, pray to thy Father which is in secret; and thy Father which seeth in secret shall reward thee openly. – Matt. 6:6

3. MAINTAIN AN ATTITUDE OF REPENTANCE

Behold, the LORD'S hand is not shortened, that it cannot save; neither his ear heavy, that it cannot hear: But your iniquities have separated between you and your God, and your sins have hid his face from you, that he will not hear. – Isaiah 59:1-2

4. MAKE FRIENDS WITH OTHERS OF LIKE FAITH

Be not deceived: evil communications corrupt good manners. – 1 Cor. 15:33

Be ye not unequally yoked together with unbelievers: for what fellowship hath righteousness with unrighteousness? and what communion hath light with darkness? – 2 Cor. 6:14

5. MODIFY YOUR SCHEDULE TO MAKE TIME FOR KINGDOM WORK

I must work the works of him that sent me, while it is day: the night cometh, when no man can work. – John 9:4

40. THE PRECIOUS BLOOD OF CHRIST

ILLUSTRATION:
[40]Recently I was sitting in a doctor's office with one of my young sons, and the nurse wanted to draw blood from him for a test. As you can imagine, he did not want to have blood taken from him. Who does? So he told me, "Dad, I can't do it. I just can't do it."

The nurse said, "Here's the deal, buddy. We've got this numbing spray. We'll spray the numbing spray on you, and then we'll stick the needle in you, and you won't even feel it."

But my son kept saying, "I can't do it. I can't do it."

Finally I said to the nurse, "Ma'am, I know what I'm about to ask you may be out of bounds, but can you stick me first? Can you do it without the numbing spray? I just need to show my son."

She said, "Yes, I'll do it. We'll keep this between us."

So I put my son on my lap, and I said, "Watch Daddy." I rolled up my sleeve and stuck my arm out. Then the nurse stuck me and drew blood. A smile came over my son's face. Yes, he was still a little nervous, but when he saw that Daddy already went through what he was about to go through, with no numbing spray, he stuck his arm out. It gave him courage.

---

[40] BRYAN LORITTS, FROM THE SERMON "THE GREAT EXCHANGE," PREACHED AT FELLOWSHIP MEMPHIS, IN MEMPHIS, TENNESSEE

In the same way, when you find yourself in the midst of hard times, look to the place where they drew Jesus' blood. Look to the cross, and there you will find rest for your souls.

1. THE BLOOD OF CHRIST CONVERTS THE LOST

And from Jesus Christ, who is the faithful witness, and the first begotten of the dead, and the prince of the kings of the earth. Unto him that loved us, and washed us from our sins in his own blood. – Rev 1:5

2. THE BLOOD OF CHRIST INVERTS OUR POSITION

That at that time ye were without Christ, being aliens from the commonwealth of Israel, and strangers from the covenants of promise, having no hope, and without God in the world: But now in Christ Jesus ye who sometimes were far off are made nigh by the blood of Christ. – Eph. 2:12-13

3. THE BLOOD OF CHRIST INSERTS US INTO GOD'S FELLOWSHIP

Take heed therefore unto yourselves, and to all the flock, over the which the Holy Ghost hath made you overseers, to feed the church of God, which he hath purchased with his own blood. – Acts 20:28

4. THE BLOOD OF CHRIST ASSERTS THE BLESSING OF FORGIVENESS

In whom we have redemption through his blood, the forgiveness of sins, according to the riches of his grace. – Eph. 1:7

5. THE BLOOD OF CHRIST EXERTS A POWERFUL INFLUENCE

And, having made peace through the blood of his cross, by him to reconcile all things unto himself; by him, I say, whether they be things in earth, or things in heaven. – Col. 1:20

6. THE BLOOD OF CHRIST SUBVERTS THE POWERS OF HELL

Forasmuch then as the children are partakers of flesh and blood, he also himself likewise took part of the same; that through death he might destroy him that had the power of death, that is, the devil. – Heb. 2:14

41. THE CROWNS OF CHRIST

Then came Jesus forth, wearing the crown of thorns, and the purple robe. And Pilate saith unto them, Behold the man! – John 19:5

ILLUSTRATION:

[41][The disciples] had seen the strong hands of God twist the crown of thorns into a crown of glory, and in hands as strong as that they knew themselves safe. They had misunderstood practically everything Christ had ever said to them, but no matter: the thing made sense at last, and the meaning was far beyond anything they had dreamed. They had expected a walkover, and they beheld a victory; they had expected an earthly Messiah, and they beheld the Soul of Eternity.

1. A CROWN OF MOCKERY

Then Pilate therefore took Jesus, and scourged him. And the soldiers platted a crown of thorns, and put it on his head, and they put on him a purple robe, And said, Hail, King of the Jews! and they smote him with their hands.

---

[41] DOROTHY L. SAYERS, "THE TRIUMPH OF EASTER," IN THE MAN BORN TO BE KING.

Pilate therefore went forth again, and saith unto them, Behold, I bring him forth to you, that ye may know that I find no fault in him. Then came Jesus forth, wearing the crown of thorns, and the purple robe. And Pilate saith unto them, Behold the man! – John 19:1-5

2. A CROWN OF MAJESTY

But we see Jesus, who was made a little lower than the angels for the suffering of death, crowned with glory and honour; that he by the grace of God should taste death for every man. – Heb. 2:9

3. A CROWN OF MONARCHY

And I saw heaven opened, and behold a white horse; and he that sat upon him was called Faithful and True, and in righteousness he doth judge and make war. His eyes were as a flame of fire, and on his head were many crowns; and he had a name written, that no man knew, but he himself. And he was clothed with a vesture dipped in blood: and his name is called The Word of God. And the armies which were in heaven followed him upon white horses, clothed in fine linen, white and clean. And out of his mouth goeth a sharp sword, that with it he should smite the nations: and he shall rule them with a rod of iron: and he treadeth the winepress of the fierceness and wrath of Almighty God. And he hath on his vesture and on his thigh a name written, KING OF KINGS, AND LORD OF LORDS. – Rev. 19:11-16

42. CHRIST'S DOCTRINE

ILLUSTRATION:

[42]On October 19, 2010, a test was conducted at the Institute for Business and Home Safety in Richburg, South Carolina. Researchers constructed two 1,300-square-foot houses inside a $40 million laboratory and then observed how a simulated hurricane would impact the homes.

The first home was built according to conventional standards. The second home included reinforcement straps that connected every level of the building, from the foundation all the way to the roof. Then the researchers turned on giant fans, creating gusts of wind up to 110 miles per hour (equal to a category 3 hurricane). In the first two experiments, which lasted under ten minutes, both homes survived the intense winds. But when they tried a third experiment, turning on the fans for more than ten minutes, the conventional home began to shake and then collapsed. In contrast, the home with the floors and roof reinforced to the foundation sustained only cosmetic damage.

Tim Reingold, an engineer working on the experiment, summarized the results with a pointed question: "The bottom line you have to ask yourself is, which house would you rather be living in?"

We could ask the same question about our faith. Do we want to build the foundation of our lives on what we think is true, or do we want to make sure we believe the same

---

[42] *BBC NEWS*, "US RESEARCHERS CREATE HURRICANE TO TEST HOUSES," (10-19-10)

doctrine that Jesus Himself believed and taught? Only one of these will see you through the storm.

1. HIS DEITY

Who being the brightness of his glory, and the express image of his person, and upholding all things by the word of his power, when he had by himself purged our sins, sat down on the right hand of the Majesty on high. – Heb. 1:3

2. HIS HUMANITY

But made himself of no reputation, and took upon him the form of a servant, and was made in the likeness of men: And being found in fashion as a man, he humbled himself, and became obedient unto death, even the death of the cross. – Phil. 2:7-8

3. HIS MINISTRY

How God anointed Jesus of Nazareth with the Holy Ghost and with power: who went about doing good, and healing all that were oppressed of the devil; for God was with him. – Acts 10:38

4. HIS SUFFERINGS

Yet it pleased the LORD to bruise him; he hath put him to grief: when thou shalt make his soul an offering for sin, he shall see his seed, he shall prolong his days, and the pleasure of the LORD shall prosper in his hand. He shall see of the travail of his soul, and shall be satisfied: by his knowledge shall my righteous servant justify many; for he shall bear their iniquities. Therefore will I divide him a portion with the great, and he shall divide the spoil with the strong; because he hath poured out his soul unto death: and he was numbered with the transgressors; and he bare the sin of many, and made intercession for the transgressors. – Isaiah 53:10-12

5. HIS MESSAGE

That whosoever believeth in him should not perish, but have eternal life. For God so loved the world, that he gave his only begotten Son, that whosoever believeth in him should not perish, but have everlasting life. For God sent not his Son into the world to condemn the world; but that the world through him might be saved. He that believeth on him is not condemned: but he that believeth not is condemned already, because he hath not believed in the name of the only begotten Son of God. – John 3:15-18

6. HIS PRIESTHOOD

By so much was Jesus made a surety of a better testament. And they truly were many priests, because they were not suffered to continue by reason of death: But this man, because he continueth ever, hath an unchangeable priesthood. Wherefore he is able also to save them to the uttermost that come unto God by him, seeing he ever liveth to make intercession for them. For such an high priest became us, who is holy, harmless, undefiled, separate from sinners, and made higher than the heavens; Who needeth not daily, as those high priests, to offer up sacrifice, first for his own sins, and then for the people's: for this he did once, when he offered up himself. For the law maketh men high priests which have infirmity; but the word of the oath, which was since the law, maketh the Son, who is consecrated for evermore. – Heb. 7:22-28

7. HIS RETURN

For if we believe that Jesus died and rose again, even so them also which sleep in Jesus will God bring with him. For this we say unto you by the word of the Lord, that we which are alive and remain unto the coming of the Lord shall not prevent them which are asleep. For the Lord himself shall descend from heaven with a shout, with the voice of the archangel, and with the trump of God: and the dead in Christ shall rise first: Then we which are alive and remain shall be caught up together with them in the clouds, to meet the Lord in the air: and so shall we ever be with the Lord. Wherefore comfort one another with these words. – 1 Thess. 4:14-18

43. JESUS' FOOTSTEPS – PART 1

ILLUSTRATION:

[43]Many years ago when the children were small, we went for a little drive in the lovely English countryside, and there was some fresh snow. I saw a lovely field with not a single blemish on the virgin snow. I stopped the car, and I vaulted over the gate, and I ran around in a great big circle striding as wide as I could. Then I came back to the kids, and I said, "Now, children, I want you to follow in my footsteps. So I want you to run around that circle in the snow, and I want you to put your feet where your father put his feet."

Well, David tried and couldn't quite make it. Judy, our overachiever, was certain she would make it; she couldn't make it. Pete, the little kid, took a great run at it, put his foot in my first footprint and then strode out as far as he could and fell on his face. His mother picked him up as he cried.

She said to me, "What are you trying to do?"

I said, "I'm trying to get a sermon illustration."

I said, "Pete, come here." I picked up little Peter and put his left foot on my foot, and I put his right foot on my foot. I said, "Okay, Pete, let's go." I began to stride one big stride at a time with my hands under his armpits and his feet lightly on mine.

---

[43] STUART BRISCOE, "WHY CHRIST HAD TO DIE," PREACHING TODAY, TAPE NO. 163.

Well, who was doing it? In a sense, he was doing it because I was doing it. In a sense there was a commitment of the little boy to the big dad, and some of the properties of the big dad were working through the little boy.

In exactly the same way, in our powerlessness we can't stride as wide as we should. We don't walk the way we should. We don't hit the target the way we ought. It isn't that at every point we are as bad as we could be. It's just that at no point are we as good as we should be. Something's got to be done.

1. THROUGH THE WATERS OF BAPTISM

Then cometh Jesus from Galilee to Jordan unto John, to be baptized of him. But John forbad him, saying, I have need to be baptized of thee, and comest thou to me? – Matt. 3:13-14

And it came to pass in those days, that Jesus came from Nazareth of Galilee, and was baptized of John in Jordan. And straightway coming up out of the water, he saw the heavens opened, and the Spirit like a dove descending upon him: And there came a voice from heaven, saying, Thou art my beloved Son, in whom I am well pleased. – Mark 1:9-11

Know ye not, that so many of us as were baptized into Jesus Christ were baptized into his death? Therefore we are buried with him by baptism into death: that like as Christ was raised up from the dead by the glory of the Father, even so we also should walk in newness of life. – Romans 6:3-4

2. THROUGH THE WILDERNESS OF TEMPTATION

Then was Jesus led up of the Spirit into the wilderness to be tempted of the devil....Then the devil leaveth him, and, behold, angels came and ministered unto him. – Matt. 4:1, 11

For we have not an high priest which cannot be touched with the feeling of our infirmities; but was in all points tempted like as we are, yet without sin. – Heb. 4:15

3. TO THE HOUSE OF WORSHIP

And he came to Nazareth, where he had been brought up: and, as his custom was, he went into the synagogue on the sabbath day, and stood up for to read. – Luke 4:16

Not forsaking the assembling of ourselves together, as the manner of some is; but exhorting one another: and so much the more, as ye see the day approaching. – Heb. 10:25

I was glad when they said unto me, Let us go into the house of the LORD. – Psalms 122:1

4. THROUGH THE FIELDS OF SERVICE

And the King shall answer and say unto them, Verily I say unto you, Inasmuch as ye have done it unto one of the least of these my brethren, ye have done it unto me. – Matt. 25:40

And I will very gladly spend and be spent for you; though the more abundantly I love you, the less I be loved. – 2 Cor. 12:15

5. ON THE MOUNTAIN OF PRAYER

And it came to pass in those days, that he went out into a mountain to pray, and continued all night in prayer to God. – Luke 6:12

Ask, and it shall be given you; seek, and ye shall find; knock, and it shall be opened unto you. – Matt. 7:7

Pray without ceasing. – 1 Thess. 5:17

44. JESUS' FOOTSTEPS – PART 2

ILLUSTRATION:
[44]Steve Lohr writes in the New York Times:

Mr. Jobs made a lot of money over the years, for himself and for Apple shareholders. But money never seemed to be his principal motivation. One day in the late 1990s, Mr. Jobs and I were walking near his home in Palo Alto. Internet stocks were getting bubbly at the time, and Mr. Jobs spoke of the proliferation of start-ups, with so many young entrepreneurs focused on an "exit strategy," selling their companies for a quick and hefty profit.

"It's such a small ambition and sad really," Mr. Jobs said. "They should want to build something, something that lasts."

If you want to really build something that lasts, learn to follow Jesus.

1. THROUGH THE GARDEN OF DESPAIR

And he came out, and went, as he was wont, to the mount of Olives; and his disciples also followed him. And when he was at the place, he said unto them, Pray that ye enter not into temptation. And he was withdrawn from them about a stone's cast, and kneeled down, and prayed, Saying,

---

[44] STEVE LOHR, *"The Power of Taking the Big Chance," N.Y. Times* (10-8-11)

Father, if thou be willing, remove this cup from me: nevertheless not my will, but thine, be done. And there appeared an angel unto him from heaven, strengthening him. – Luke 22:39-43

When my father and my mother forsake me, then the LORD will take me up. – Psalms 27:10

2. TO THE CROSS OF SUFFERING

Though he were a Son, yet learned he obedience by the things which he suffered. – Heb. 5:8

Wherefore Jesus also, that he might sanctify the people with his own blood, suffered without the gate. – Heb. 13:12

3. THROUGH THE VALLEY OF DEATH

Yea, though I walk through the valley of the shadow of death, I will fear no evil: for thou art with me; thy rod and thy staff they comfort me. – Psalms 23:4

4. TO THE THRONE OF GOD

Lift up your heads, O ye gates; and be ye lift up, ye everlasting doors; and the King of glory shall come in. – Psalms 24:7

To him that overcometh will I grant to sit with me in my throne, even as I also overcame, and am set down with my Father in his throne. – Rev. 3:21

45. THE HEAD OF CHRIST

ILLUSTRATION:

[45]As a kid, I loved Mission Sundays, when missionaries on furlough brought special reports in place of a sermon .... There is one visit I've never forgotten. The missionaries were a married couple stationed in what appeared to be a particularly steamy jungle. I'm sure they gave a full report on churches planted or commitments made or translations begun. I don't remember much of that. What has always stayed with me is the story they shared about a snake.

One day, they told us, an enormous snake—much longer than a man—slithered its way right through their front door and into the kitchen of their simple home. Terrified, they ran outside and searched frantically for a local who might know what to do. A machete-wielding neighbor came to the rescue, calmly marching into their house and decapitating the snake with one clean chop.

The neighbor reemerged triumphant and assured the missionaries that the reptile had been defeated. But there was a catch, he warned: It was going to take a while for the snake to realize it was dead.

A snake's neurology and blood flow are such that it can take considerable time for it to stop moving even after decapitation. For the next several hours, the missionaries were forced to wait outside while the snake thrashed about, smashing furniture and flailing against walls and windows,

---

[45] CAROLYN ARENDS, "SATAN'S A GONER: A LESSON FROM A HEADLESS SNAKE," *Christianity Today* (FEBRUARY, 2011)

wreaking havoc until its body finally understood that it no longer had a head.

Sweating in the heat, they had felt frustrated and a little sickened but also grateful that the snake's rampage wouldn't last forever. And at some point in their waiting, they told us, they had a mutual epiphany.

I leaned in with the rest of the congregation, queasy and fascinated. "Do you see it?" asked the husband. "Satan is a lot like that big old snake. He's already been defeated. He just doesn't know it yet. In the meantime, he's going to do some damage. But never forget that he's a goner."

The story [still] haunts me because I have come to believe it is an accurate picture of the universe. We are in the thrashing time, a season characterized by our pervasive capacity to do violence to each other and ourselves. The temptation is to despair. We have to remember, though, that it won't last forever. Jesus has already crushed the serpent's head. [And while Jesus has crushed Satan's head, His own head brings us multiple blessings.]

1. AN UNRESTED HEAD

And Jesus said unto him, Foxes have holes, and birds of the air have nests; but the Son of man hath not where to lay his head. – Luke 9:58

2. AN ANOINTED HEAD

And being in Bethany in the house of Simon the leper, as he sat at meat, there came a woman having an alabaster box of ointment of spikenard very precious; and she brake the box, and poured it on his head. – Mark 14:3

3. A THORN CROWNED HEAD

And the soldiers platted a crown of thorns, and put it on his head, and they put on him a purple robe, And said, Hail, King of the Jews! and they smote him with their hands. – John 19:2-3

4. A BOWED HEAD

When Jesus therefore had received the vinegar, he said, It is finished: and he bowed his head, and gave up the ghost. – John 19:30

5. AN UNCOVERED HEAD

And the napkin, that was about his head, not lying with the linen clothes, but wrapped together in a place by itself. – John 20:7

6. A BEAUTIFUL HEAD

His head and his hairs were white like wool, as white as snow; and his eyes were as a flame of fire. – Rev. 1:14

7. A CROWNED HEAD

His eyes were as a flame of fire, and on his head were many crowns; and he had a name written, that no man knew, but he himself. – Rev. 19:12

46. THE HEADSHIP OF CHRIST

ILLUSTRATION:

[46]A number of years ago, when I was playing in a friendly men's softball game, the umpire made a call that incensed our coach. My coach didn't agree with the ump's interpretation of a specific league rule. The game stopped, and a heated discussion ensued. Finally, the ump sighed as he pulled a rulebook from his back pocket and proceeded to read page 27, paragraph 3b, section 1.

"As you can clearly see," he concluded, "this rule means that my call must stand." Unconvinced, my coach yelled, "But you're not interpreting that rule correctly." To which the ump replied, "Uh, excuse me, I think I should know: I wrote the rulebook." After an awkward silence, my coach walked back to the bench, shaking his head and pointing to the ref as he told us, "Get ahold of that guy. He wrote the rulebook!"

Throughout his ministry, Jesus didn't just affirm and endorse the words of Scripture; he talked and acted like he had AUTHORED the Scriptures. He lived with the authority of the One who wrote the "rulebook."

1. THE HEAD OF THE CORNER

This is the stone which was set at nought of you builders, which is become the head of the corner. – Acts 4:11

---

[46] MATT WOODLEY, *The Gospel of Matthew: God With Us* (INTERVARSITY PRESS, 2011), PP. 68-69

2. THE HEAD OF EVERY MAN

But I would have you know, that the head of every man is Christ; and the head of the woman is the man; and the head of Christ is God. – 1 Cor. 11:3

3. THE HEAD OF THE CHURCH

For the husband is the head of the wife, even as Christ is the head of the church: and he is the saviour of the body. – Eph. 5:23

4. THE HEAD OF ALL PRINCIPALITY AND POWER

And ye are complete in him, which is the head of all principality and power. – Col. 2:10

5. THE HEAD OF ADMINISTRATION

But speaking the truth in love, may grow up into him in all things, which is the head, even Christ. – Eph. 4:15

6. THE HEAD OVER ALL THINGS

And hath put all things under his feet, and gave him to be the head over all things to the church, Which is his body, the fulness of him that filleth all in all. – Eph. 1:22-23

7. THE HEAD OF CHRIST IS GOD

But I would have you know, that the head of every man is Christ; and the head of the woman is the man; and the head of Christ is God. – 1 Cor. 11:3

47. JESUS IS KING

ILLUSTRATION:

[47]Travel back 200 years in Christian history to John Newton, the slave-trader-turned-pastor and hymn writer. He would receive almost unbelievable answers to his prayers because he believed in what he called "large asking." When explaining what he meant, Newton would often cite a legendary story of a man who asked Alexander the Great to give him a huge sum of money in exchange for his daughter's hand in marriage. Alexander agreed, and told the man to request of Alexander's treasurer whatever he wanted. So, the father of the bride went and asked for an enormous amount. The treasurer was startled and said he could not give out that kind of money without a direct order. Going to Alexander, the treasurer argued that even a small fraction of the money requested would more than serve the purpose.

"No," replied Alexander, "let him have it all. I like that fellow. He does me honor. He treats me like a king and proves by what he asks that he believes me to be both rich and generous."

Newton concluded: "In the same way, we should go to the throne of God's grace and present petitions that express honorable views of the love, riches, and bounty of our King."

1. THE APPOINTED KING

---

[47] *unknown*

But thou, Bethlehem Ephratah, though thou be little among the thousands of Judah, yet out of thee shall he come forth unto me that is to be ruler in Israel; whose goings forth have been from of old, from everlasting. – Micah 5:2

2. THE ANOINTED KING

But unto the Son he saith, Thy throne, O God, is for ever and ever: a sceptre of righteousness is the sceptre of thy kingdom. Thou hast loved righteousness, and hated iniquity; therefore God, even thy God, hath anointed thee with the oil of gladness above thy fellows. – Heb. 1:8-9

3. THE ASSAULTED KING

Then Pilate therefore took Jesus, and scourged him. And the soldiers platted a crown of thorns, and put it on his head, and they put on him a purple robe, And said, Hail, King of the Jews! and they smote him with their hands. – John 19:1-3

4. THE ASCENDED KING

The God of our fathers raised up Jesus, whom ye slew and hanged on a tree. Him hath God exalted with his right hand to be a Prince and a Saviour, for to give repentance to Israel, and forgiveness of sins. And we are his witnesses of these things; and so is also the Holy Ghost, whom God hath given to them that obey him. – Acts 5:30-32

5. THE ACCLAIMED KING

And he was clothed with a vesture dipped in blood: and his name is called The Word of God. And the armies which were in heaven followed him upon white horses, clothed in fine linen, white and clean. And out of his mouth goeth a sharp sword, that with it he should smite the nations: and he shall rule them with a rod of iron: and he treadeth the winepress of the fierceness and wrath of Almighty God. And he hath on his vesture and on his thigh a name written, KING OF KINGS, AND LORD OF LORDS. – Rev. 19:13-16

48. CHRIST'S RETURN

ILLUSTRATION:

[48]We decided to let our three-year-old son record the message for our home answering machine. The rehearsals went smoothly: "Mommy and Daddy can't come to the phone right now. If you'll leave your name, phone number, and a brief message, they'll get back to you as soon as possible."

Then came the test. I pressed the record button and our son said sweetly, "Mommy and Daddy can't come to the phone right now. If you'll leave your name, phone number, and a brief message, they'll get back to you as soon as Jesus comes."

1. PROMISED BY JESUS

And if I go and prepare a place for you, I will come again, and receive you unto myself; that where I am, there ye may be also. – John 14:3

2. DECLARED BY ANGELS

Which also said, Ye men of Galilee, why stand ye gazing up into heaven? this same Jesus, which is taken up from you into heaven, shall so come in like manner as ye have seen him go into heaven. – Acts 1:11

3. FORETOLD BY PETER

---

[48] CHRISTIAN READER, "KIDS OF THE KINGDOM."

But the day of the Lord will come as a thief in the night; in the which the heavens shall pass away with a great noise, and the elements shall melt with fervent heat, the earth also and the works that are therein shall be burned up. – 2 Peter 3:10

4. DESCRIBED BY PAUL

But I would not have you to be ignorant, brethren, concerning them which are asleep, that ye sorrow not, even as others which have no hope. For if we believe that Jesus died and rose again, even so them also which sleep in Jesus will God bring with him. For this we say unto you by the word of the Lord, that we which are alive and remain unto the coming of the Lord shall not prevent them which are asleep. For the Lord himself shall descend from heaven with a shout, with the voice of the archangel, and with the trump of God: and the dead in Christ shall rise first: Then we which are alive and remain shall be caught up together with them in the clouds, to meet the Lord in the air: and so shall we ever be with the Lord. Wherefore comfort one another with these words. – 1 Thess. 4:13-18

5. COMMENDED BY JAMES

Be patient therefore, brethren, unto the coming of the Lord. Behold, the husbandman waiteth for the precious fruit of the earth, and hath long patience for it, until he receive the early and latter rain. Be ye also patient; stablish your hearts: for the coming of the Lord draweth nigh. – James 5:7-8

49. JESUS THE TEACHER

ILLUSTRATION:

[49]In the 19th century Charles Bradlaugh, a prominent atheist, challenged a Christian man to debate the validity of the claims of Christianity. The Christian was Hugh Price Hughes, an active soul-winner who worked among the poor in the slums of London. Hughes told Bradlaugh he would agree to the debate on one condition.

Hughes said, "I propose to you that we each bring some concrete evidences of the validity of our beliefs in the form of men and women who have been redeemed from the lives of sin and shame by the influence of our teaching. I will bring 100 such men and women, and I challenge you to do the same."

Hughes then said that if Bradlaugh couldn't bring 100, then he could bring 20. He finally whittled the number down to one. All Bradlaugh had to do was to find one person whose life was improved by atheism, and Hughes—who would bring 100 people improved by Christ—would agree to debate him. Bradlaugh withdrew!

1. JESUS TAUGHT THE TRUTH OF GOD

And ye shall know the truth, and the truth shall make you free. – John 8:32

2. JESUS TAUGHT THE WORDS OF GOD

---

[49] D. JAMES KENNEDY AND JERRY NEWCOMBE, WHAT IF JESUS HAD NEVER BEEN BORN? (THOMAS NELSON, 1997), P. 189

God is a Spirit: and they that worship him must worship him in spirit and in truth. – John 4:24

3. JESUS TAUGHT THE LOVE OF GOD

For God so loved the world, that he gave his only begotten Son, that whosoever believeth in him should not perish, but have everlasting life. – John 3:16

4. JESUS TAUGHT THE WILL OF GOD

For I came down from heaven, not to do mine own will, but the will of him that sent me. – John 6:38

5. JESUS TAUGHT THE WAY OF GOD

Jesus saith unto him, I am the way, the truth, and the life: no man cometh unto the Father, but by me. – John 14:6

6. JESUS TAUGHT THE DOCTRINE OF GOD

Jesus answered them, and said, My doctrine is not mine, but his that sent me. – John 7:16

7. JESUS TAUGHT WITH THE POWER OF GOD

And they were astonished at his doctrine: for his word was with power. – Luke 4:32

8. JESUS TAUGHT WITH THE AUTHORITY OF GOD

For he taught them as one having authority, and not as the scribes. – Matt. 7:29

50. JESUS IS PERFECT – PART 1

ILLUSTRATION:

[50]Cattle-rustling is a major problem in Uganda. The Ugandan army daily attempts to reunite cattle with their owners. The biggest difficulty lies in proving ownership. This article recounts how one elderly lady settled the issue:

The BBC's Nathan Etungu witnessed the process beginning in a village north of Mbale. He told the BBC's Network Africa that when an elderly woman stood before the herd a remarkable thing happened. She called her cows by name and to the amusement of the soldiers, as each cow heard her voice, it lifted its head and then followed her.

As far as the army was concerned, it was as strong a proof of ownership as one could find.

1. JESUS HAS PERFECT CHARACTER

I am the good shepherd, and know my sheep, and am known of mine. – John 10:14

2. JESUS HAS PERFECT KNOWLEDGE

I am the good shepherd, and know my sheep, and am known of mine. – John 10:14

---

[50] HEARD ON *Paul Harvey* (2-28-03); "UGANDAN COWS KNOW THEIR NAMES," BBC.COM, (2-25-03);

3. JESUS HAS A PERFECT SACRIFICE

As the Father knoweth me, even so know I the Father: and I lay down my life for the sheep. – John 10:15

4. JESUS HAS PERFECT OBEDIENCE

No man taketh it from me, but I lay it down of myself. I have power to lay it down, and I have power to take it again. This commandment have I received of my Father. – John 10:18

5. JESUS HAS A PERFECT GIFT

And I give unto them eternal life; and they shall never perish, neither shall any man pluck them out of my hand. – John 10:28

6. JESUS HAS A PERFECT KEEPING

And I give unto them eternal life; and they shall never perish, neither shall any man pluck them out of my hand. – John 10:28

7. JESUS HAS PERFECT UNITY

I and my Father are one. – John 10:30

51. JESUS IS PERFECT – PART 2

ILLUSTRATION:

[51]In January of 2006, Ed Lorenz bowled the third perfect game of his life. A few minutes later, he suffered a heart attack and died.

The 69-year-old retiree had started bowling in 1957, and had recorded his two other 300 games during a 1-week stretch in 2004. His per-game average for his last full season was 223, and in 2005 he was inducted into the Kalamazoo Metro Bowling Association Hall of Fame.

According to Lorenz's bowling partner, Johnny D. Masters, it was a fitting end to his life. "If he could have written a way to go out," said Johnny, "this would have been it."

While a perfect score in bowling is certainly impressive, it fails in comparison to living a perfect life like Jesus did.

1. HIS PERFECT WORK

But I have greater witness than that of John: for the works which the Father hath given me to finish, the same works that I do, bear witness of me, that the Father hath sent me. – John 5:36

2. HIS PERFECT FORGIVENESS

---

[51] ANDREW HARD, "TALK ABOUT GOING OUT ON TOP," *FoxNews.com* (1-3-06)

Then said Jesus, Father, forgive them; for they know not what they do. And they parted his raiment, and cast lots. – Luke 23:34

3. HIS PERFECT CARE

Casting all your care upon him; for he careth for you. – 1 Peter 5:7

4. HIS PERFECT VICTORY

But thanks be to God, which giveth us the victory through our Lord Jesus Christ. – 1 Cor. 15:57

5. HIS PERFECT PROVISION

I can do all things through Christ which strengtheneth me. – Phil. 4:13

6. HIS PERFECT GRACE

But let patience have her perfect work, that ye may be perfect and entire, wanting nothing. – James 1:4

7. HIS PERFECT OPERATION

If this man were not of God, he could do nothing. – John 9:33

52. JESUS' COMPASSION

ILLUSTRATION:

[52]John was a priest in Kronstadt, Russia, in the mid-to late-nineteenth century. That was a time and place of dirty marketplaces. Imperial Russia was decadent, rotting beneath its own weight, and the streets were dangerous, rife with poverty and depravity. Crime ran amok. Alcoholism was rampant. Prostitutes crowded the corners, thieves the alleys. There was no safe place, so most people who weren't part of that world didn't venture out into it. Most of the clergy, used to a life of privilege and status, used what waning powers they had to insulate themselves from the widespread peril and hardship.

Not so Father John. His daily practice was to don his robe and descend into the meanest part of the city. He'd walk among the addicts and the predators, the whores and the thieves, the orphans and the widows, and he did it with healing in his wings. He would find the most broken and dissolute man or woman he could track down, lying in a gutter or standing on a street corner. He would cup their chin in his large hand and lift their face so they were looking directly

---

[52] MARK BUCHANAN, *Your Church Is Too Safe* (ZONDERVAN, 2012), PP. 88-89

in his eyes. "This," he would say, meaning this way of life, this means of survival, this condition I found you in, "this is beneath your dignity. You were created to house the glory of the living God."

Father John, in his lifetime, was called the Pastor of All Russia. And everywhere he went, revival came with him.

1. FOR THE WORLD'S PAIN

And Jesus went forth, and saw a great multitude, and was moved with compassion toward them, and he healed their sick. – Matt. 14:14

And as they departed from Jericho, a great multitude followed him. And, behold, two blind men sitting by the way side, when they heard that Jesus passed by, cried out, saying, Have mercy on us, O Lord, thou Son of David. And the multitude rebuked them, because they should hold their peace: but they cried the more, saying, Have mercy on us, O Lord, thou Son of David. And Jesus stood still, and called them, and said, What will ye that I shall do unto you? They say unto him, Lord, that our eyes may be opened. So Jesus had compassion on them, and touched their eyes: and immediately their eyes received sight, and they followed him. – Matt. 20:29-34

2. FOR THE WORLD'S CONFUSION

But when he saw the multitudes, he was moved with compassion on them, because they fainted, and were scattered abroad, as sheep having no shepherd. – Matt. 9:36

3. FOR THE WORLD'S LONELINESS

And Jesus, moved with compassion, put forth his hand, and touched him, and saith unto him, I will; be thou clean. – Mark 1:41

4. FOR THE WORLD'S HUNGER

Then Jesus called his disciples unto him, and said, I have compassion on the multitude, because they continue with me now three days, and have nothing to eat: and I will not send them away fasting, lest they faint in the way. – Matt 15:32

5. FOR THE WORLD'S SORROW

Now when he came nigh to the gate of the city, behold, there was a dead man carried out, the only son of his mother, and she was a widow: and much people of the city was with her. And when the Lord saw her, he had compassion on her, and said unto her, Weep not. – Luke 7:12-13

Thank You for Your Investment in this Book!

Barry L. Davis, D.Min.

If we can help you with more ministry resources please feel free to visit us at:

www.pastorshelper.com

Made in the USA
Charleston, SC
30 January 2013